Modern Basketry

Modern Basketry
From The Start

BARBARA MAYNARD

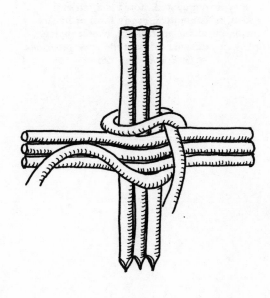

LONDON : G. BELL AND SONS, LTD.

ISBN 0 7135 1733 6

Printed in Great Britain by
Redwood Press Limited, Trowbridge, Wiltshire

To my Husband, Ron,
who has always given me the
greatest encouragement possible.

Acknowledgements

I WOULD like to thank some people for helping me with this book. Firstly, Mrs Tudor, of Trumpington, Cambs., who taught me the first steps of basketry. She instilled in me the rudiments of good craftsmanship and tradition, and laid down the foundations of my knowledge. Secondly, Miss Diana Rixon, who sat for such long hours to make the illustrations so clear and easy to follow. Thirdly, Mrs Sharp for the lovely photographs and Mrs Dinah Millson for the final typing. And finally, my family, including my Mother-in-law and Kathleen, who allowed me to write instead of char, and my sons who patiently (sometimes) acknowledged that Mummy needed peace and quiet while she was in her writing 'igloo'.

Contents

Plates

(between pages 116 and 117)

Introduction

I STARTED basketry in 1964 after a period of being housebound with infant sons, but it was not until I started playing with willow and then hedgerow stuffs that I really became enamoured. Now I encourage all my pupils to try willow and experience its wonderful properties for themselves.

The aim of this book is to set down all the information that I have gradually 'picked up' and about which so little has been written. I have tried to write it down just as I would say it in class, so I hope that you will bear with some of the repetition in this book. I think that it is necessary, just as it is in class.

I have used the basket maker's language throughout the book. They are nearly all Anglo-Saxon words which have been passed down to us. I find them fascinating and I hope that you will too. I hope that you will gradually learn to use them, especially if you are a teacher of basketry.

May I particularly ask you, when you are using this book to read all the relevant paragraphs to each bit of work, and not just to follow the illustrations. I have tried to write down all the snags and pitfalls and helpful wrinkles that I have gained through my own teaching and practical experience and I want to pass them on to you. I hope that even experienced basket makers will find the chapter of Hints and Tips useful.

I would like to encourage you to persevere over the difficult beginnings of willow basketry and to go on to make some really lovely things of your own design.

Try very hard to get *some* instruction—basketry is a subject that is very difficult to learn without actually seeing the moves.

Ickleton,   B. G. M.

April, 1972

1. Tools

THE TOOLS required for basketry are not expensive or very numerous, and some of them can be made at home. (Figure 1.)

Bodkin. A sharp piercing tool (the true meaning of the word bodkin). Used for all branches of basketry, for piercing the stuff, and for forming a channel when rods have to be inserted, e.g. when staking up, cramming off or weaving away. The advanced basket maker will have a large and a small but the beginner could manage with an old screwdriver honed down to a point. Curved bodkins are available but are seldom used.

Shears. Essential for willow and hedgerow basketry. The garden secateurs will do just as well as long as they are *sharp*. Cane workers would find them easier to use than side-cutters for anything thicker than No. 8 cane.

Knife. Also essential, especially for willow and hedgerow. Must have a point for pricking up (see page 5) and must be kept very, very sharp. If you are unable to sharpen your own knife it is best to use a modern one with removable blades. I find that a STANLEY knife is excellent. Apart from pricking up, it is used for slyping and picking off.

Rapping Iron. A blade of iron, used for rapping down the sides of the basket to keep it level, or for close randing. An old metal workers file will do or even a small (4 oz) hammer.

Side Cutters. For cane only (it squeezes and bruises willow and hedgerow). Used for cutting into lengths and for picking off. Can be used for making a point on a stake if you haven't a sharp knife.

Round Nose Pliers. Again for cane workers only. Used for nipping the cane at the upsett and border, which helps the stakes to turn down without cracking.

I

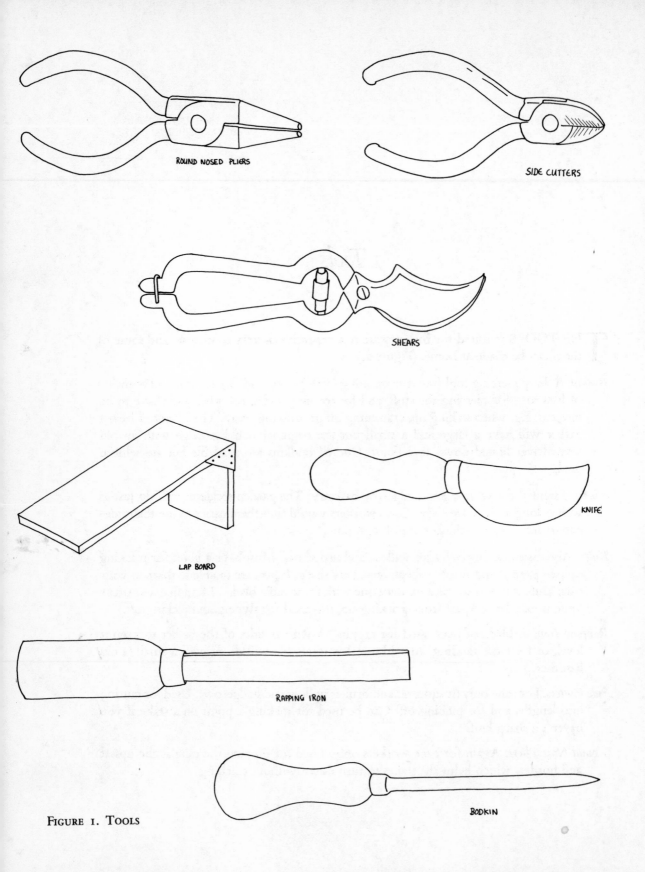

ROUND NOSED PLIERS

SIDE CUTTERS

SHEARS

LAP BOARD

KNIFE

RAPPING IRON

BODKIN

FIGURE 1. TOOLS

Screwbox. For squarework in both willow and cane. They can be bought but the commercial ones are rather small and only suitable for very light, dainty work, and not strong enough to withstand the pull of the work. Easily made at home to suit your own size and requirements. (See Figure 2.) You will need two pieces of wood, say 2 in × 2 in (or 2 in × 3 in for, a larger one) and about 15 in long, with two holes drilled right through both of them so that they exactly correspond, about 4 in from each end. Two 5 in coach bolts are placed in the holes and screwed up with wing nuts.

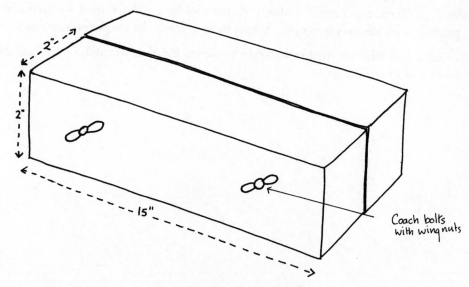

Coach bolts with wing nuts

FIGURE 2. THE SCREWBLOCK

Measuring Tape. Any tape or measuring stick will do. Remember that the measurement of a basket is taken on the *inside* for the length and breadth but on the outside for the height.

Board, Lap-Board or Plank. Used for tying or pinning the basket to, in order to keep it steady and firm while working on the siding and border. Board and plank are just pieces of soft wood and a lap-board is easily made, but take care not to make the slope too great.

Stones, Weights, Flat-Iron. Used for the same purpose as the board and lap-board, but is much easier to manage as it gives greater freedom of movement. I prefer this method. Paint stones, from garden or seashore, in gay colours with poster or water paints then varnish them. The great advantage of the stones is that there is always one of the right size to fit the basket of the moment.

Bradawl. Used for pinning the work, through the centre of the base, to the work board.

Singeing Lamp. Used for singeing off 'whiskers' of canework, but hardly necessary nowa-
days as the cane is of better quality than it used to be. Again, a home made one can
be made very simply. Punch a hole in the top of a tin that has a tight fitting lid and
thread a wick (a piece of piping cord will do) through the hole. Use only methylated
spirits—paraffin (and candles) will blacken the cane. The burner from a child's
chemistry set will do very well. (So sons do have their uses!)

Clothes Pegs. These are a useful addition to the tool-box and are used for securing base
pairing or handle wrapping etc., if you have to leave the work for any reason.

Nails. Galvanised nails are used in basketry to secure handles, wrapping etc. Available in
packets of assorted sizes.

2. Explanation of some Terms & Processes

AT THE end of this book I have given a 'dictionary' of technical terms used in basketry but some of them require more detailed explanation and I have, therefore, grouped them separately in this chapter so that you can refer to them easily.

1. SLYPE

The name given to the method of pointing the end of a piece of cane or willow.

With a *sharp* knife, make a cut, starting about 1 in from the end of the rod, as if you were sharpening it. Turn the cane 90° (or a ¼ of the way round) and cut again, so that it leaves a pointed end. If it doesn't quite end in a point, then trim the end so that it does. This kind of cut is made specially so that the cane is only cut half way round and the remainder is left with the outer surface still on. A long slype would start about 1½ in–2 in back from the point and is used for staking up and handle bows etc. (Figure 3.)

2. PRICKING-UP (OR DOWN)

This technique is used for willow and hedgerow only. It is used when a very sharp bend in the rod is required, e.g. at the upsett or border. Insert the point of the knife well into the stakes, but not right through, just beyond the edge of the base or about ¼ in–½ in above the siding, for the border. (Figure 4A.) Now twist the knife in the cut, AND AT THE SAME TIME, with your left hand, bend the stake upwards (or downwards). This breaks down the tubular effect of the rod, at this particular point, and allows it to turn without cracking. (Figure 4B.)

It is not necessary to keep the pricked-up rods in the bent position. As each stake is pricked-up it may be allowed to fall into its original position—having once made the prick-up, it will bend easily again at this point.

3. BYE-STAKING

The process of adding a second stake beside the side of a main stake, to give extra strength and stability. Nearly all cane baskets need a bye-stake, but they are seldom used

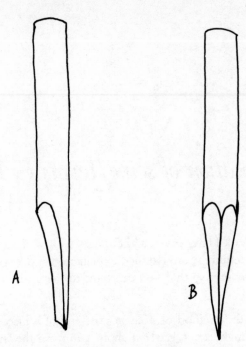

FIGURE 3. THE SLYPE

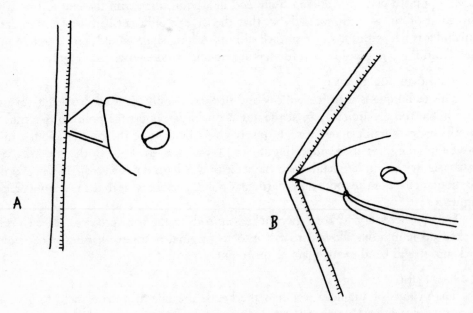

FIGURE 4. PRICKING-UP

with willow and hedgerow. This is for the simple reason that a thicker stake can be selected which will be no thicker at the border.

The bye-stake is sometimes the length of the height of the basket, or can continue on to make a border with double stakes.

Cut the bye-stakes the length required, slype one end, and insert them into the weaving, usually the waling of the upsett, to the *right* of the side stake, and in the same channel as the side stake. (Figure 5.)

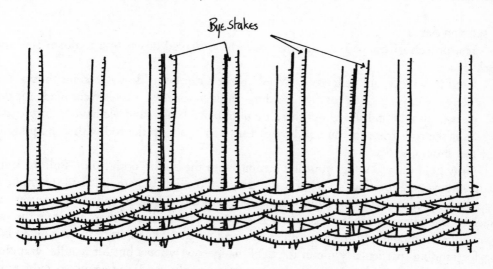

FIGURE 5. BYE-STAKING

When the siding is finished, unless the bye-stakes are carried into the border, trim any surplus protruding cane level with the last round of waling.

4. HOOPING THE STAKES

After the stakes have been bent up it is necessary to keep them in an orderly upright position, while the upsett is being done.

Either tie the stakes together at the top, or put on a hoop. Make a hoop from a piece of cane or willow rod, twisted round itself and tied into position. The hoop is then attached to the stakes, fairly near the top; secure in 2 or 3 places with string or sellotape. The size and shape of the hoop depends on the basket, and on the amount of flow that is required. The greater the amount of flow required, the larger the hoop will be in relation to the base. The hoop is either round for a round basket or oval for an oval or *square* basket; if you use a square hoop, the stakes will gather into the corners.

5 PICK-OFF

The process of tidying all the protruding ends of a basket. Try to make the cut as diagonal as possible. The cut end should lie against a stake, except for waling.

Ideally the cut should be made with a knife as this makes a much cleaner cut but you will find it easier to use side cutters for cane and shears for willow.

Pick-off willow and hedgerow as you go, as it is easier to cut when wet, and cane only after the basket, or section, is dry to allow for shrinkage.

6. SKEIN WORK

The process of using split rods that have been shaved down to a uniform size and thickness.

Used in willow and hedgerow. Whole baskets can be made with skeins, but in this book they are only used for handles or siding. In days gone by, 3 tools were made for this job, cleave, upright and shave, but these are unobtainable now and we have to improvise.

Split the rods from the butt end by slitting 1 in or so, up the rod with a sharp knife. The rod should be dry.

Now hold the rod under your left armpit, with the butt in both hands. Pull the splits apart with your 2 forefingers, at the same time controlling the amount and direction of the split by pressure with the thumbs on the sides of the rod. If the split starts to veer too much to one side, put more pressure ON THE OTHER SIDE with that thumb. Move the rod up in your hands and split the next bit, and so on to the tip. The split rods can be used like this for randing (particularly useful for thick hedgerow woods) but for handle wrapping they need to be fined down. It may be necessary to split the $\frac{1}{2}$ rod again, to reduce the width. Shave the thickness of the rod, and the pith, away from the inside, with a sharp knife, leaving the skin intact on the outside. Try to get the skeins as uniform in width as possible. The skein should now be very thin and pliable.

To use these skeins, dip in water for a few minutes and then wrap your handle. Use a 2nd as a leader.

3. Materials

CANE

CANE, CENTRE CANE, Pulp Cane, Pith Cane are all different names for the same thing. It comes from the rattan plant which grows in Asia. It is a rambling creeper and grows to fantastic lengths. The outer skin or bark has large thorns which makes harvesting very difficult. This bark is shredded away and discarded, leaving a second hard glossy skin. The skin is peeled off and cut into lengths of uniform width and thickness. It is then sold as Glossy Wrapping Cane, or a finer quality as Chair Seating Cane, both of which the basketmaker uses for decoration on the siding or for wrapping the handle.

The inside, and you can see now why it is called pith, pulp or centre cane, is factory processed to produce lengths of about 20 to 30 feet, of a completely uniform thickness throughout. This uniformity certainly makes the basket-making easier, but unfortunately it also reduces the beauty and character, or 'nature', of the material. And, of course, the processing and the importation make it very much more expensive than willow.

Cane is bought by the pound, or even a quarter of a pound in retail craft shops, and is obtainable in a range of sizes from 000 to 16. (See Figure 6 for a table of relative sizes and thickness.) Cane is available in different qualities—red (or green) tie is of fairly good quality for normal use, but use blue tie, which is the best, for exhibition or examination work. Bleached cane, or white tie, is obtainable but is even more de-natured than ever, and I do not advocate its use at all. Singapore quality cane is cheaper and darker than red tie, and the quality varies, but I usually find that it is quite suitable for beginners.

Apart from the sizes in the table we can also get handle cane in sizes of 8 mm or 10 mm and flat cane which is sometimes used for wrapping and sometimes used for decoration in the siding. This flat cane is often enamelled in lovely colours and is therefore called enamelled cane. It is used as the leader of a wrapped handle or again, for decoration in the siding. Although it is rather expensive, it is only used in small quantities and does put a bit of colour into a cane basket.

9

Modern Basketry from the Start

FIGURE 6. SIZES AND MEASUREMENTS OF CANE

Cane Size	Measurement
000	1 mm
00	$1\frac{1}{4}$ mm
0	$1\frac{1}{2}$ mm
1	$1\frac{3}{4}$ mm
2	$1\frac{7}{8}$ mm
2	2 mm
4	$2\frac{1}{4}$ mm
5	$2\frac{1}{2}$ mm
6	$2\frac{5}{8}$ mm
7	$2\frac{3}{4}$ mm
8	3 mm
9	$3\frac{1}{4}$ mm
10	$3\frac{3}{8}$ mm
11	$3\frac{1}{2}$ mm
12	$3\frac{3}{4}$ mm
13	4 mm
14	$4\frac{1}{4}$ mm
15	$4\frac{1}{2}$ mm
16	5 mm

To prepare the cane for working, soak it in hot water for a few minutes. The length of time varies, and it is difficult to lay down any set times. To weave with No. 5 for instance, would only require about a 5 minute soak, but to border down with the same cane would take a little longer. Some of the finer canes are hard and wiry and need more soaking than a thick one. The more experienced and proficient you become the less you will need to soak your cane. (I no longer need to soak No. 3 or No. 5 at all for weaving unless it is very unkind.) However, for the beginner the following table may help as a guide.

Handle cane	30 min
Nos. 12–16	20 min
Nos. 8–11	15 min
Nos. 4–7	10 min
Nos. 1–3	5 min
Nos. 0–000	Just dipped
Flat, glossy and Chair seating . . .	Just dipped

Having soaked the stuff, keep it covered with a damp cloth until it is required. It dries out very quickly, especially in central heating. If it dries out while you are working, dip it in the water again for a few moments.

No rules can be laid down as to which size of cane should be used for stakes and which should be used for weavers. It depends entirely on the size and quality of your basket.

For instance, No. 3, a fairly fine cane normally used for weaving small baskets, was used for stakes in the hat on page 151 with No. 1 as the weaving cane. And then again a shopping basket would need sturdier cane than say, a work basket of the same size.

Palembang Cane

Also of the rattan family. It is sometimes called whole cane as it is not stripped and processed. It is bought in two thicknesses only, 3–5 mm or 5–8 mm, and has to be graded like willow before starting the basket. Again like cane some of the thinner pieces are hard and wiry, while some of the thicker canes can be quite soft and pliable. Of all the basketry materials palembang is probably the hardest to use.

To prepare for use it has to be soaked in cold water overnight (longer if it is still unworkable) and wrapped to mellow for a further 2 or 3 hours. If re-soaking is necessary, for instance in preparation for turning down the border, hot water may be used for quicker results.

WILLOW BASKETRY

Very little has been written about willow basketry for the simple reason that it is a very traditional craft and the knowledge has always been passed from father to son, or from master to apprentice, in a very practical way. Perhaps this is why it has now got the reputation that it is rather difficult. This is not so at all, and it's much more of a knack that you need (in common with a lot of other crafts) and big strong hands are not at all necessary. My own hands are quite small, size 6½, and unless I have been doing some gardening or decorating, always perfectly presentable. The oil from your hands goes well with the willow and the lovely velvety smooth surface of well prepared stuff is a joy to handle.

A basket made from willow has many wonderful qualities. It is extremely strong and if well made should last about 50 to 60 years even with constant use. It will retain its colour as long as it is not left out in bright sunlight. It is also very light in weight—a good sized shopping basket would only weigh about 6 oz. It costs very much less than a similar one in cane.

Willow that is bought (that is, not the willow that is picked from the hedgerows), is called commercial willow because it is specially grown and prepared for the basket trade. There is no doubt about it that English willows are the kindest to use, and we are lucky to have it without having to import it.

The varieties grown for the trade are *Salix Triandra*, *Salic Purpurea* and *Salix Viminalis*. They can be bought as brown, buff and white. Brown has been dried with the bark on; white has been stripped of its bark before it is dried and buff has been boiled with the bark on, to allow the tannin to stain the wood, and then it is stripped and dried.

It is possible to buy small amounts of willow by the pound from some crafts suppliers, but if larger amounts are required, it is sold by the bolt or bundle. These bolts are in stated lengths of anything from 2–3 feet which would be suitable for dainty work, up to 10 feet for making heavy hampers and furniture. 4–5 foot would be the best size for a beginner and there would be enough variation out of one bolt, in the thickness of the rods to find sticks, stakes and weavers.

For the preparation of the willow, select only enough for your immediate use. Soak it overnight (brown takes a little longer) preferably in soft water, so that if it rains just leave it outside on the grass. Next morning, wrap it up in an old sack or piece of blanket that has been dipped in water and wrung out, for a further 2 or 3 hours. This mellows the willow and is just as important as the soaking. As you become more proficient with your willow-work, you will be able to cut down on the preparation time. But do see that it is well prepared and pliable before beginning work. Nothing is worse than to have your rods cracking just because they were not soaked or wrapped for long enough. All the willow that is 'waiting' to be used should be kept very carefully wrapped up in the damp blanket until it is required. If it becomes dry and begins to 'squeak', dip it for $\frac{1}{2}$ hour to restore the right condition. As long as it is kept wrapped in the damp cloth, it will remain workable for about 2 days, but any not used by then should be dried out thoroughly before re-use or storing. Willow that has been wrapped up for too long becomes greasy to the feel, and the next stage is that it will go mouldy. Willow that has been re-soaked too often will go a bad colour, but otherwise is still usable.

One of the most important things in willow work is the 'cutting out' or grading of the rods. It is essential that the bottom sticks are the thickest, and the weavers of the base are the finest, the side stakes are the next thickest and the siding is worked with the remainder. So before the basket is started, cut the required number of base sticks from the sturdiest rods. Then select the number of stakes that you want from the next thickest (plus 2 or 3 spares) and lay them aside, still covered, until they are needed. This ensures that by the time the weaving at the top of the siding is reached, the rods that are left are not thicker than the stakes. This would be disastrous for the shape and evenness of the basket as the weavers would 'govern' the stakes. The same, of course, applies to a cane basket but it is made easier for us because of the regulated sizing of the cane.

The rods for the handle roping should be the longest and yet the finest possible at the butt end, out of the whole bundle, and must have no blemishes on them at all. If your basket is to have a handle, it is as well to select these rods first, and 'hide' them until the bow is in.

Apart from the grading of willow before use, there are many other differences of working between cane and willow.

When pairing or waling, the rods must always be approximately the same length and thickness and new rods are joined in both, or all, at the same time. This is to avoid working with one thick and one thin rod, in which case the thick rod would dominate the thin and the weaving would become very uneven. Try, also, to keep all the weavers of French randing to a similar thickness and length—partly for the same reason and partly because it is such a waste to have to cut many long ones off because 5 or 6 have run out. (If only one or two run out early, perhaps because sufficient long ones weren't available, or if one breaks off, it is quite permissible to piece in, choosing a small rod equal in size to the others at this point.)

Piece in, or join, butts to butts and tips to tips for pairing, waling and ordinary randing. This means that having finished the first weaver or set of weavers at the butts, start the second one, or set, with the butts also. There are other ways of joining in but I have always found that this is the best and neatest method and the simplest for beginners. If piecing in is necessary because of a blemish or a broken rod, as with the French randing, choose a rod that is the same thickness at this point, cut it to the same length and let it run out with the others. If you are half way through the weaving rods make sure that you put the new one in the right way round. Often a broken rod can be trimmed and re-inserted.

One of the main differences between willow and cane is that, whereas the cane weaver passes round the stake with a curve, willow kinks slightly. This is one of the reasons why a willow basket is so much more firm and rigid, and for the same reason, if the weaving has to be undone, *never* re-use those same weavers again, they will only go back into the same positions as before and you will have gained nothing. Select new ones, they are cheap enough.

Figure 7 shows the difference between cane and willow positions while weaving.

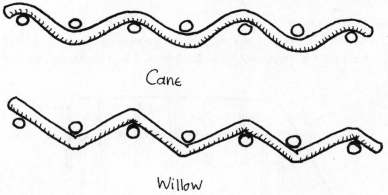

FIGURE 7. THE DIFFERENCE BETWEEN CANE AND WILLOW RANDING

4. Weaves & Borders

IN ORDER to begin your basketwork it is necessary to learn the basic weaves and borders. If you have done no basketry at all and are unable to get any tuition, make yourself a 'practice board'. With this board you will be able to practise each weave thoroughly, before using it on your basket. Furthermore, the illustrations in the book will look more like the work on the board than on the actual basket.

Practice Board (See Figure 8)

You will need a piece of peg board, any size or shape, but about 10 in × 14 in would be ideal. Cut a number of pegs about 3 in long from No. 15 cane or some odd pieces of

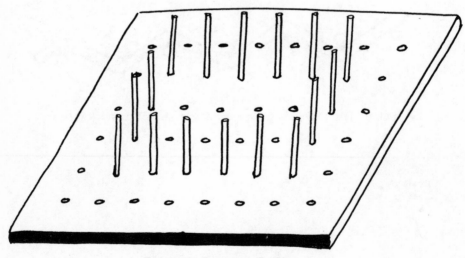

FIGURE 8. PRACTICE BOARD

similar sized willow and insert them into the holes of the peg board. Do not put them too close to the edge of the board. Allow them to protrude about 1 in underneath and see that they are quite firmly fixed into the board. Form an oblong or square with the pegs. It is now ready for you to try out your weaves. Keep your board until you are quite sure you have mastered all the weaves. By working to the top of the pegs and inserting some border stakes, it can be used for practising the borders also.

WALING

Waling is the weave used when strength is required. All well made English baskets have waling at the top and the bottom and often in the middle as well. If your basket begins to run out of shape, a band of waling can often help to pull it back and tidy it up. Waling is generally put on with three weavers but it can be done with 4, 5 or even 6. It is referred to as a three-rod wale or a four-rod wale etc. We often use more weavers at the bottom of the basket, at the point that we call the upsett, so that the basket stands on a ridge.

Start your waling by inserting 3 weavers in 3 consecutive spaces between the stakes (or pegs of your practice board). N.B. Your weavers will either be willow rods of a set length, or uncertain lengths of cane. Do not allow these weavers to be too long, about 7 ft–8 ft is plenty, or they get into such a muddle. It is not at all necessary for the canes to be all the same length.

Take the left hand weaver and pass it in front of two stakes and then behind the next one (over the top of the other two weavers) so that the long end now comes out of the next or fourth space. (Figure 9.)

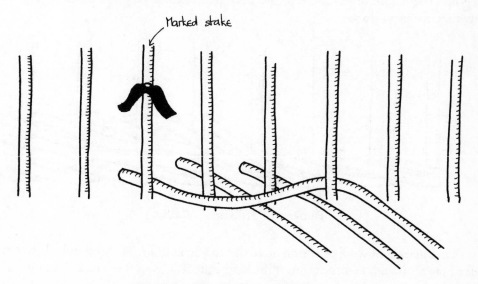

FIGURE 9. THE START OF WALING

Continue in this way, always using the left hand weaver (you will therefore use each weaver in turn) until you are round to the space BEFORE the first one that you used. (Figure 10.)

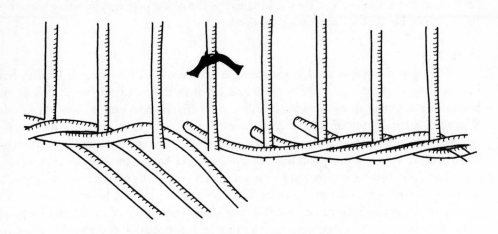

FIGURE 10. THE END OF THE FIRST ROUND

At this point, if we are using cane, every time round we have to do a step-up. This is to prevent a 'spiralled' effect. (Figure 11.) Willow and hedgerow workers do not use this step-up. The nature of the material, because the thickness varies so much, makes it unnecessary for us to do so.

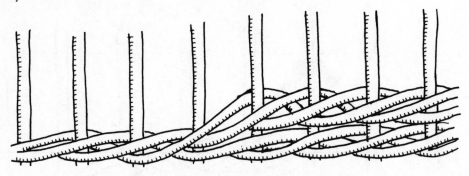

FIGURE 11. 'SPIRALLED' WALING

Tie a marker of wool or cotton on to the very next stake. That is the one between the left of the short ends and the right of the long ends. This is so that you will know on subsequent rounds exactly where to start your step up.

1. Take the *right* hand weaver and pass it in front of two stakes and behind the next one, Figure 12.

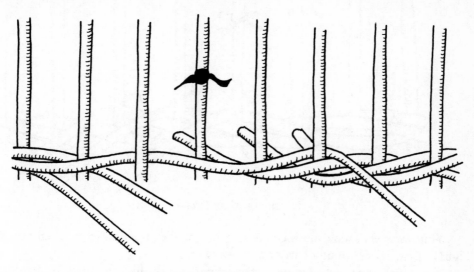

FIGURE 12. THE STEP-UP (1)

2. Take the middle one and pass that in front of two stakes and behind the next one, Figure 13.

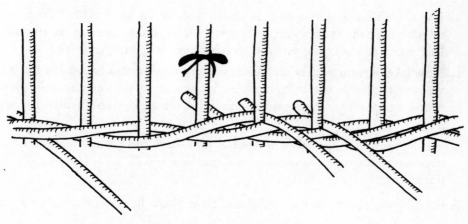

FIGURE 13. THE STEP-UP (2)

3. Take the left hand one and pass it in front of two stakes and behind the next one, Figure 14.

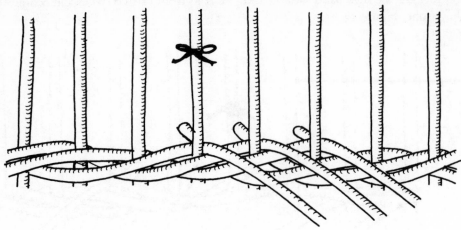

FIGURE 14. THE STEP-UP (3)

Your weavers should now be coming out of the same spaces as when you started, Figure 14, with one round of working in between.

Now start your second round of working exactly like the first, i.e. pass each left hand weaver in front of two stakes and behind the next one until you come to the marked stake again. Repeat the step-up at this point.

Continue with as many rounds as you like, each time doing the step-up, and then on the last round, finish off like this:

1. Use the left hand weaver once more, in front of two and behind the next one, which will be the marked one, and cut it off leaving about 4 in—to be trimmed off later when you are quite sure that you have got it right. (Figure 15.)

2. Now take the next weaver on the left and pass it in front of two stakes and behind the next, but before you bring it out to the front, lift up the top cane of the previous round, and pass the weaver underneath and so out to the front. Trim off as before. (Figure 16.)

3. The last weaver is also taken in front of two stakes and behind one, and is passed underneath the top two canes of the previous round, on its way to the front. (Figure 17.)

N.B. All your weavers of the final round should now lie under two other weavers.

Four or Five Rod Wale

When you are using a four rod wale, pass the left hand weaver in front of three stakes and behind the next one. Similarly, with 5 or 6 weavers it will be in front of 4 and 5 respectively, and then behind the next one.

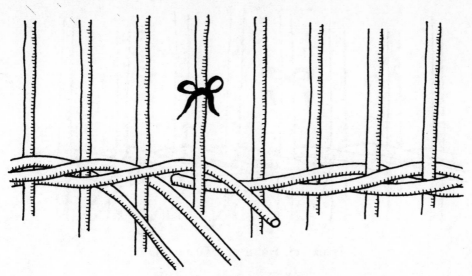

FIGURE 15. FINISH OF WALING

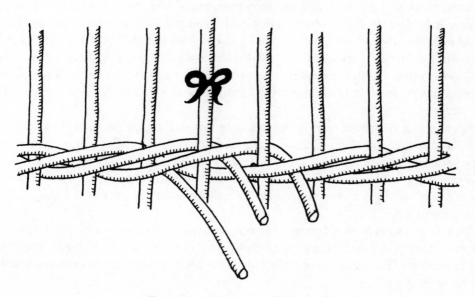

FIGURE 16. FINISH OF WALING (2)

We usually use a 4, 5 or 6 rod wale at the upsett of a basket, i.e. when the basket changes from going out to going up, so that it makes a thick ridge for the basket to stand on. Uusually only one round of this thicker weave is done.

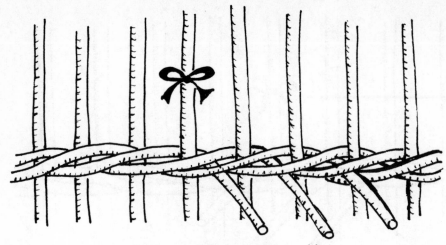

FIGURE 17. FINISH OF WALING (3)

When using 4 weavers in willow, insert the ends into the previous work, but when using cane, bend 2 long ones in half and loop them round 2 of the stakes. This is to avoid too many ends. And similarly, when 5 weavers are required, loop 2 pieces round and have one odd one, and with 6 loop 3 pieces round 3 stakes. You will find that the weavers will not go round consecutive stakes or you would have 2 weavers coming out of some of the spaces, so each time one stake must be missed out in between. If you are in doubt about this, put 4 ends in and join them into 2 pairs behind the stakes. You will soon get an idea of the pattern.

Having made one round with 4 weavers, drop one so that you can continue with only 3, thus: let one go round the marked stake and cut it off to about 6 in, do a normal step up with the remaining three canes. (Figure 134.) Weave the 6 in cut end in later.

When using willow drop any one of the four weavers whenever it is convenient. We don't have to abide by the same rules for willow as we do for cane because of the 'nature' of the stuff.

With 5 or 6 weavers it is better to do one complete round and finish off. Finish off as for the 3 rod wale, but continue on to under 3 canes of the previous round, and then under 4 and so on. Then start your 3 rod wale as a separate thing and not even necessarily in the same place.

Joining In

To join in a new piece of cane, wait until the first one to be replaced is the left hand one. Pull this short end back with your left thumb and slip the new piece in to lay beside it. You should now have one end to the inside and one end to the outside. Don't attempt to make them both lie to the inside or you will weaken the join. (Figure 18.)

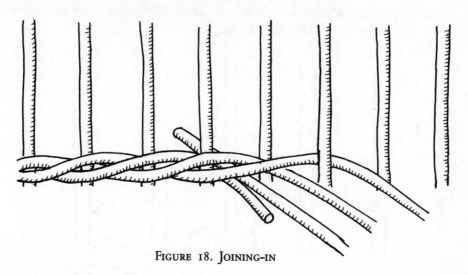

FIGURE 18. JOINING-IN

Don't join in a new cane on the step-up! The step-up will become bumpy and muddled. Go back a few spaces and join in there.

Join in all the willow rods at the same time, and don't forget that you join in butts to butts and tips to tips.

PAIRING

Pairing is put on with 2 weavers and is used particularly to weave round and oval bases. We sometimes refer to pairing as 'putting on a pair'.

Start by bending your cane roughly in the middle and looping it round a stake, Figure 19A, or by inserting the 2 ends in 2 consecutive spaces, Figure 19B.

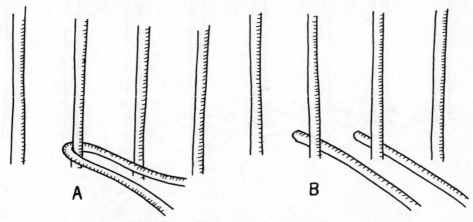

FIGURE 19. THE START OF PAIRING

Take the left hand weaver in front of one stake (over the top of the other) and behind one stake and back to the front again, Figure 20.

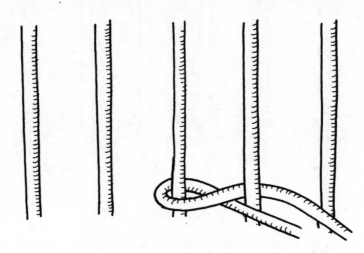

FIGURE 20. PAIRING

Continue in this way for as many rounds as you require. There is no step-up to worry about. Joining in can be done in exactly the same way as for waling, and this is the best for beginners. (Figure 21.) For more advanced students there is a better way of joining in your pairing rods.

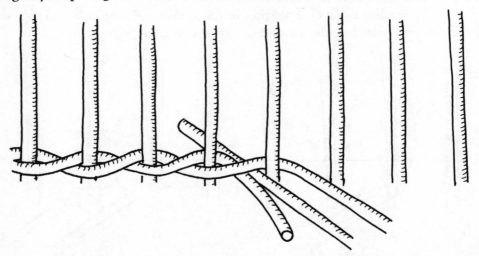

FIGURE 21. JOINING-IN PAIRING

Joining In, Advanced Method

Instead of pulling the old end back and inserting the new one on the right of the old, lift the old weaver up slightly and insert the new one underneath it and to the LEFT of the old end. (Figure 22.) When continuing to pair, pass the new weaver over the top of the old end. It should look rather like a granny knot. (Figure 23.) It has the great advantage that each of the ends finally lie against a stake and not against each other. This join is only suitable for pairing.

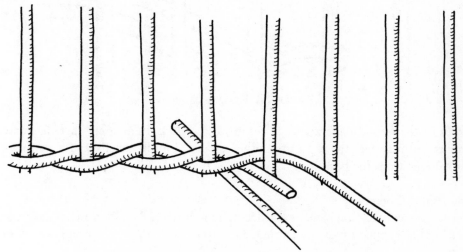

FIGURE 22. JOINING-IN PAIRING—ADVANCED METHOD (1)

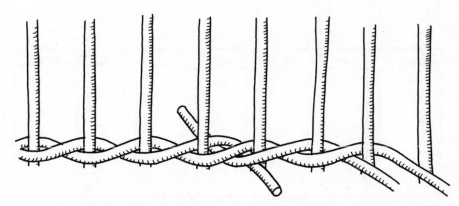

FIGURE 23. JOINING-IN PAIRING—ADVANCED METHOD (2)

Reverse Pairing (Figure 24)

Used on an oval base to prevent twisting. Exactly the same as pairing but the weavers are held at the back of the work. The left hand weaver will come behind the first stake and

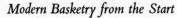

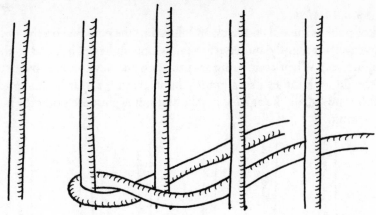

FIGURE 24. REVERSE PAIRING

in front of the second stake and then return to the back. Remember that the weaver in use must still pass over the top of the other weaver. Join in exactly as for pairing but it must be done from the back.

Chain Pairing (Figure 25)

Used on an oval cane base, or for decoration on the siding. Consists of one round of pairing and one round of reverse pairing. Be careful to see that each round does not overtake the other.

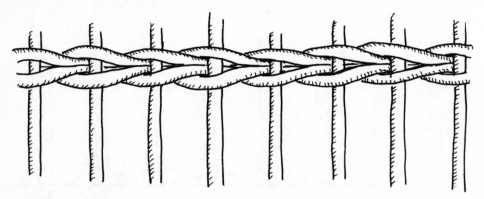

FIGURE 25. CHAIN PAIRING

FITCHING (Figure 26)

This weave is used after leaving a space in your basket. See photo of bird cage and bells etc. It looks like reverse pairing when it is done, but the method of working is different.

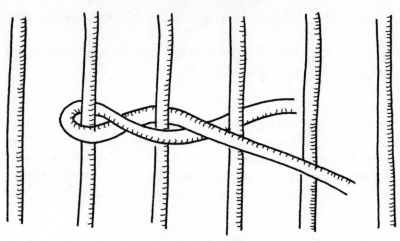

FIGURE 26. FITCHING (1)

Bend your weaver round, as for pairing, roughly in the centre, and loop it round a stake, at the height above the previous working that you require.

Now, pass the left hand weaver in front of one stake and behind the next and out to the front, but this time it goes UNDERNEATH the other weaver. In fact the two weavers should be grasped in the fingers of the right hand and twisted firmly towards you. Then the left hand one (or the underneath one) is merely passed round the back of the next stake. This ensures a good strong weave which grips the stake firmly and tightly. This is necessary after leaving a gap in the work.

If your stakes are very wide apart and the 'twist' of the fitch does not seem to hold the stakes firmly in place, twist the weavers twice before passing the underneath one round the back of the next stake. (Figure 27.)

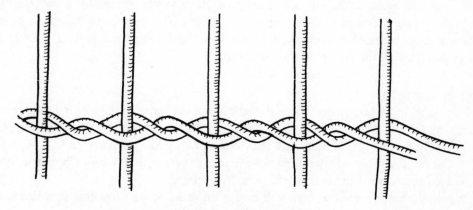

FIGURE 27. FITCHING (2)

You may shape your basket at the same time as your fitching, but take great care to keep it all even.

You may cross the stakes over, if they are double, while you are fitching, but see that you have plenty of practice with plain fitching first.

Fancy Fitching (Figure 28)

A very attractive siding can be put on with fitching using extra bye stakes. You will require twice as many bye-stakes as there are main stakes. They are best if they are cut from cane a couple of sizes smaller than the main stakes. If you are using willow then these bye-stakes could well be made out of spare tip ends. Cut them approximately 3 in longer than the depth of the space that you are having. Insert these bye stakes into the waling

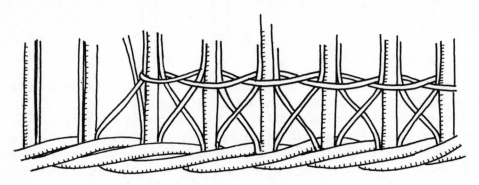

FIGURE 28. FANCY CROSS FITCHING

before the space, one on each side of each stake. Loop your fitching cane round a stake and catch in with that loop—the right bye-stake of the previous stake, AND the left bye-stake of the next main stake. You will now have three pieces of cane (or willow) in the loop of the weaver. Complete the fitching stroke. Repeat at the second stake, and so on. This is not easy to describe on paper, try to follow the diagram and look at Plate 6. Be very sure to keep all the crosses in the same order.

Joining In (Figure 29)

To join in, in fitching, insert the end of the new cane between the top and the bottom weavers, on the left side of the one to be replaced (this should be on top of the other) and then pass it over the old end. It should look like a granny knot. (Figure 30.)

It is better, however, to try not to have to join in on the first round. Choose weavers that will go right round the basket with a little to spare.

When working in willow, you will find it easier to do your fitching in a fine cane. Even if you want your basket to be all willow, still do the first fitching round in cane,

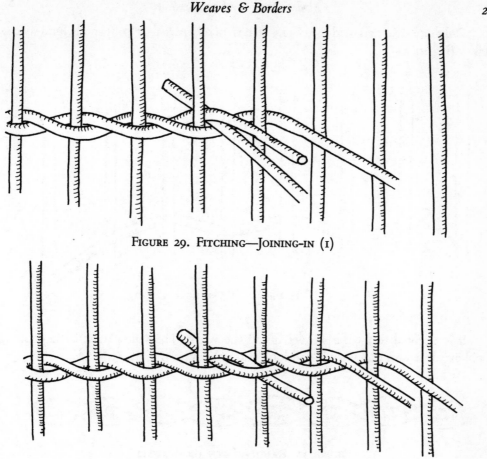

FIGURE 29. FITCHING—JOINING-IN (1)

FIGURE 30. FITCHING—JOINING-IN (2)

then a second fitch in willow. Then, when you have worked a bit more of your basket and it is all quite firm, you can cut the cane away.

To start the fitching in willow, bend a long thin rod at about 9 in from the tip end, and use this as 2 weavers. Then when the short end runs out, join in with a new one that will run out with the other.

RANDING

This is the simplest of all the weaves to learn to do, but at the same time it is the most difficult in relation to keeping the work even. There are many different forms of randing. In this book we shall learn to do ordinary randing and French randing. Ordinary randing is used on all square bases and on the siding of cane baskets. It is not generally suitable for the siding in willow work; for this we use French randing.

Only one weaver is used at a time, and it is merely passed in front and behind successive stakes. (Figure 31.)

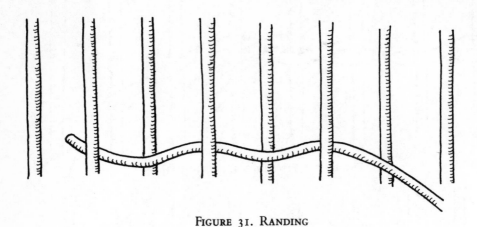

FIGURE 31. RANDING

It is essential to let the weaver do all the work. The stakes must be kept straight. Looking down on the work it will look perfectly even. (Figure 32.)

FIGURE 32. RANDING SEEN FROM ABOVE

At the same time this is the weave to use for shaping your work. You can pull your basket out or push it in, as you wish, while you are randing.

It will help you to make or keep your shape, if you hold the stake that the weaver is passing in front of. Hold it firmly in the thumb and first and second fingers of the left hand, until the weaver is finally in position. Do not grip it too firmly, that will only make your fingers ache, merely keep that stake in the position that you want it to be in. If you want your basket to flow out then pull the stakes towards you, but if you want your basket to go in then push the stakes slightly away from you. Do not exaggerate, a little experimenting will soon get it right. Be sure to keep hold of the stake until the weaver is quite settled. See Plate 1, which shows the position of the hands.

Randing is very much simpler when done on an odd number of stakes. To this end, we should always work with an odd number if possible. However if you have an even number it will mean that when you have gone right round your basket and you are back to the first stake, you will find that the weaver will pass in front of the same stake as it did before, instead of going behind that one on the second round.

The method of working with an even number of stakes is as follows. (Figure 33.)

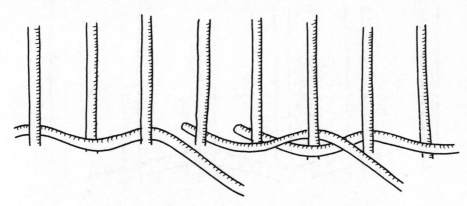

FIGURE 33. RANDING WITH AN EVEN NUMBER OF STAKES

Put in one round of randing. Add a second weaver, starting in the next space to the LEFT of the first one. Work one round with the second weaver. Now revert to the first weaver for the 3rd round, and to the second one for the 4th round, and so on. You must never let either weaver overtake the other.

Joining In (Figure 34)

To join in a new cane in randing, both the old and the new canes should lie at the back of the same stake, to be trimmed off later.

FIGURE 34. JOINING-IN FOR RANDING

French Randing

This form of randing is used for the siding of a willow or hedgerow basket and is not suitable for cane.

One weaver is required for each stake.

The method of working is as follows:

1. Insert the butt of one weaver in between any two stakes.

2. Pass that weaver in front of the next stake to the right, and behind the next one, and out to the front, and leave it. (Figure 35.)

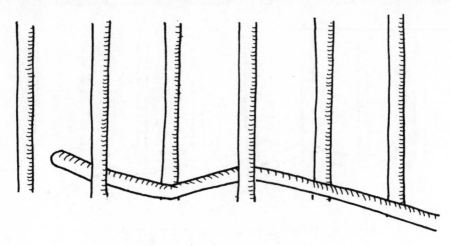

FIGURE 35. FRENCH RANDING (1)

3. Take a second weaver and insert its butt in the space to the left of where you first started.

4. Weave this one in front of one stake to the right and behind the next and out to the front again and leave it. (Figure 36.)

5. Continue in this way until you have used all the weavers and there is a weaver coming out of each space. Check! When putting the last 2 in, be very careful not to cross over the first ones. Lift up the first weavers and pass the last ones underneath them.

6. This is one complete round. Each round of this work is complete in itself and need not be started where the previous one finished. In fact sometimes it is a good thing not to, especially if you're a bit shaky on the finishing point.

7. For the next and subsequent rounds, starting with any weaver you like, pass it in front of one stake and behind the next and out to the front as you did for the first round. (Figure 37.)

8. Now the next weaver on the left and use it in exactly the same way. You will now find that 2 of these spaces have *two* weavers coming from them, one from the previous round and the one you have just used. (Figure 38.) This is perfectly in order, and you will sort it out at the end of the round.

9. Continue with the randing strokes all the way round until you come to the space with 2 weavers in it.

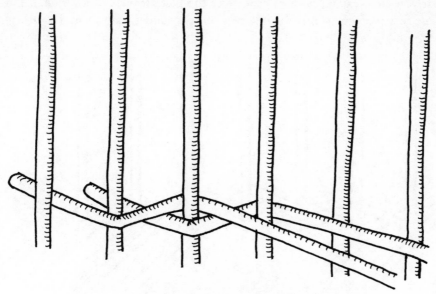

FIGURE 36. FRENCH RANDING (2)

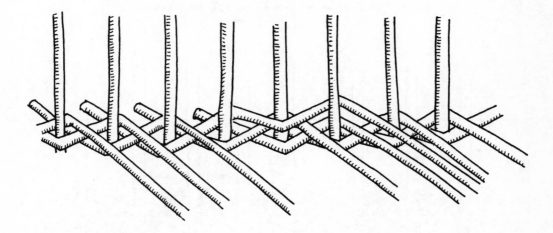

FIGURE 37. THE SECOND ROUND OF FRENCH RANDING (1)

10. To finish the round, take the bottom weaver from the next space and weave in front of one and behind one with that.

11. Last of all take the next one at the bottom, that is the second of the double ones, and weave in front of one and behind one taking great care not to allow the one

that you are weaving with to cross over the first weavers of the round. Lift up those first weavers so that the last ones can pass underneath them. (Figure 39.)

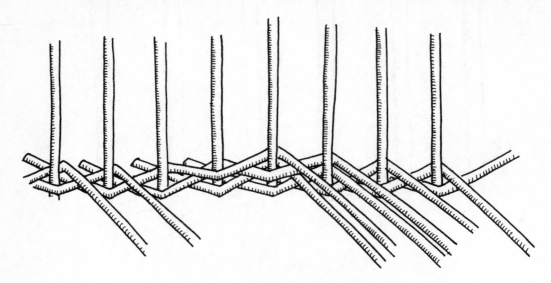

FIGURE 38. THE SECOND ROUND OF FRENCH RANDING (2)

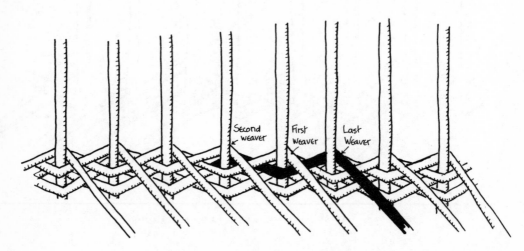

FIGURE 39. FINISHING FRENCH RANDING

Continue with these rounds, always completing one round before starting the next, until the side is as high as you want it, or until the weaving rods have run out to the tips.

Then tuck each weaver to the inside of the basket to rest behind the next stake, and trim them.

Always remember to control your stakes by holding them with the thumb and the first and second fingers of the left hand, while the weaver passes in front of that stake.

French randing can be started on the first round by taking each weaver in front of 2 stakes and behind one. This gives the appearance of one round of waling and is useful when you are starting the second band of French randing. One word of warning, don't use this method until you are quite sure that you know what you are doing.

SLEWING

Slewing is another weave more suitable for willow and hedgerow than cane, as it can only be done with rods that taper to a point. (Randing done with 2 canes of the same size is really double randing.)

It is a very economical weave and is to be recommended if you are short of stuff. It is used for the siding. It is essential to have an odd number of stakes.

2 *Rod Slew*

1. Place a butt in between two stakes and rand until you have used up half the rod.
2. Take a second rod and place the butt in between two stakes and on top of the first rod. (Figure 40.)

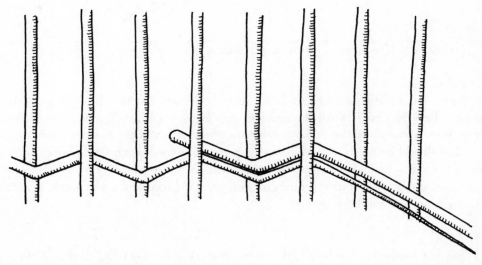

FIGURE 40. SLEWING (1)

3. Weave both these rods together until the one at the bottom runs out.

4. Join in a new rod as before, behind the same stake that the under one's tip ran out.

5. Weave the second and third rods together until the second one runs out. (Figure 41.)

6. Join in a new one etc.

7. Continue in this way until the siding is as high as you want it.

8. See that you leave all the tip ends on the inside of the basket.

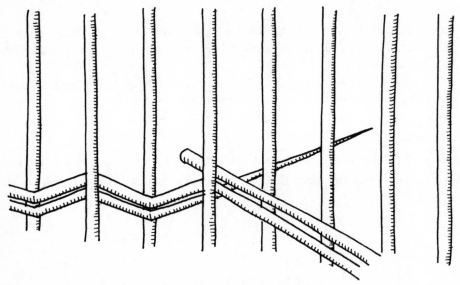

FIGURE 41. SLEWING (2)

3 or 4 Rod Slew

As for the 2 rod slew, but join in the new rod when the first is $\frac{1}{3}$ (or $\frac{1}{4}$) used, and a third when the first is $\frac{2}{3}$ (or $\frac{1}{2}$ then you will need a 4th at $\frac{3}{4}$) used. From then on always join in a new rod, butt end, on the top of the others as the bottom tip runs out.

Care should be taken in slewing to keep the combined strengths of both, or all the weavers, less than the stakes, or you will stand little chance of controlling the shape of your basket. I find that a 2 rod slew is quick and easy and a 3 rod slew is just about as much as I can manage, and still keep it even.

BORDERS

Borders are used to finish off and neaten the work at the top edge, the edges of covers, or lids, and sometimes underneath the work, and then it is called a foot border.

There are three main types of border—Trac (or track), Rod and Plait, all of which have many variations. There are other borders that are either rather advanced or not used very often. Certainly these will be enough to get you started. There is also a Scallop border which is very frail, and comes undone very easily; I do not recommend it at all.

The border is made with the end of the side stakes, but remember, that while the stakes are upright they are still *stakes* and must be kept *straight* and not be allowed to bend in and out or become kinked. But once the stake has been turned down, it becomes the weaver and then does all the work of 'going in and out'.

Before the border is started, take great care to see that the siding is level at the top. If it is not, then rap it down with the iron and make sure it *is* level, or the border will be uneven in height. It shouldn't happen with cane because of the evenness of the material, but with willow and hedgerow it is quite usual.

Before the border is started make sure that the material is damp enough. Many good baskets have been spoiled when the stakes cracked at the border because they weren't damp enough. Willow often requires a dip in the tub at this stage (about 15 mins will resoak the stuff, as long as it was only partially dried out).

TRAC BORDERS

This is the simplest of the borders and, if evenly woven, looks extremely attractive. It is not really suitable for shopping baskets or other baskets that are going to receive a lot of wear. It is often used in conjunction with a ledge that will hold a lid.

When using willow it is advisable to prick-down first (or kink the stakes over the edge of the thumb nail if the rods are fine). The stakes are measured and pricked-down at a uniform height all round the basket, to ensure an even border. The height required will depend on the thickness of the stakes and the number of strokes to the border.

For caneworkers, the 'elbow' where the stake is first bent down is more rounded, but they must still be of a uniform height all round the basket. It is possible to adjust the height of part of a *cane* trac border after it is finished.

Be very careful to keep the stakes straight and upright to the point of the elbow, or if they are deliberately slanted to the right or the left, or inwards or outwards, each must slant exactly the same amount, and then only from the edge of the border.

Trac Border No. 1 (Figure 42)

Bend down one stake and pass it in front of the next stake and behind the next, leaving the end to the inside of the basket.

This simple trac is used as a foot border in willow or at the edge of a ledge in cane or willow. It can also be used as a follow-on or back-trac.

Finish by tucking the last one in to follow the pattern. Trim the ends with a slanting cut, making quite sure that each end is lying firmly against its final stake.

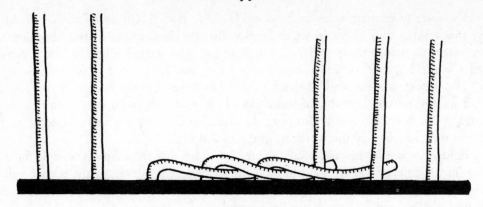

FIGURE 42. TRAC BORDER NO. 1

Trac Border No. 2 (Figure 43)

Just the same as number 1, but take each stake in front of the next 2 stakes, and tuck in and trim behind the third.

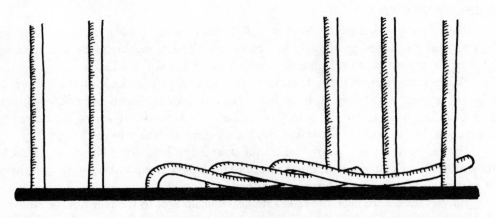

FIGURE 43. TRAC BORDER NO. 2

Trac Border No. 3 (Figure 44)

Bend down the first stake and pass it behind one stake and in front of the next 2, and then tuck it in behind the next one. Continue with each one, saying to yourself 'Behind one, in front of two and tuck it in', as you do it.

Finish the last 3 stakes in exactly the same way, even though the stakes which they are to go in front of are already turned down. The last one of all will have to pass underneath the 'elbow' of the first stake before going in front of 2 and tucking in. Be sure to tuck in next to the base, as all the others are.

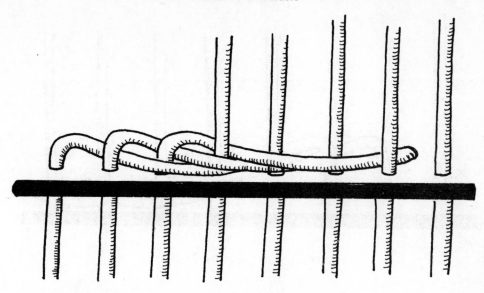

FIGURE 44. TRAC BORDER NO. 3

This is a favourite border when using a manufactured base, with cane. You will find it easier to finish the last 3 strokes if the FIRST 3 or 4 stakes are pushed up a little in order to let the last stake pass under them easily. Pull these stakes back into position afterwards.

Trac Border No. 4 (Figure 45)

Turn down the first stake about ¾ in from the border and pass this stake behind one, in front of one, behind one, in front of one, and then tuck it in behind the next stake, to be trimmed there later.

Repeat this with each stake in turn, even with the last few, although they will have to pass in front of and behind stakes that have been already turned down.

The number of in and out strokes can be increased, in which case the stakes must be turned down higher to start with.

Trac Border No. 5 (Figure 46)

Turn down the first stake about ¾ in from the border and pass it behind 2 stakes, in front of 2 stakes, then tuck it in. Repeat all the way round, finishing as before, by following the pattern out to the end.

Trac Border No. 6

Turn down the first stake at about 1¼ in from the border and pass it in front of 3 stakes, behind 2, in front of 3 and tuck it in behind the next. Continue all the way round, finishing as before.

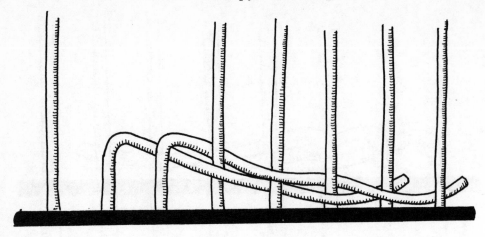

FIGURE 45. TRAC BORDER NO. 4

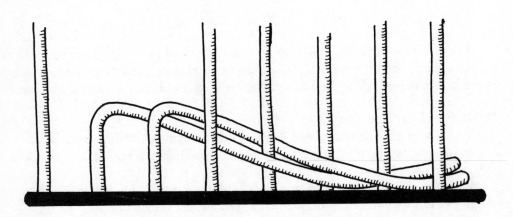

FIGURE 46. TRAC BORDER NO. 5

It can be seen by now that trac borders can be put on to any pattern and depth. They can also be used with double stakes. When using double stakes with willow, prick-down the right hand or inner one, $\frac{1}{4}$ in lower than the left, to allow it to sit happily under the left one.

It is not necessary to always turn the stakes down behind the next one first. They may pass in front first, and then go behind.

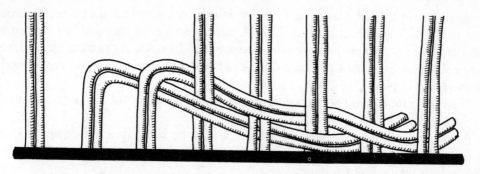

FIGURE 47. TRAC BORDER NO. 4, USING DOUBLE STAKES OF CANE

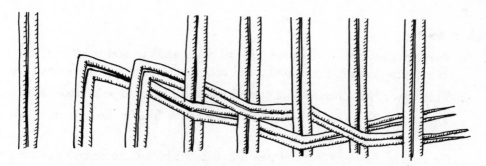

FIGURE 48. TRAC BORDER NO. 4, USING DOUBLE STAKES OF WILLOW
AND SHOWING LOWER AND UPPER 'ELBOW'

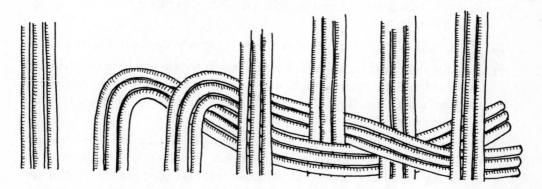

FIGURE. 49. TRAC BORDER USING TREBLE STAKES

ROD BORDERS

Again a simple border used, far more by willow basket makers than cane. Variations are, 2-rod, which is seldom used, 3-rod, the most common of them all, used when the border is to be no thicker than the side weaving, e.g. hamper, lid borders etc. A lovely sturdy border can be made by using 2 three-rod borders together, i.e. a rod border with a follow-on rod border. (See Plate 22.)

Then there are 4, 5 and 6-rod borders which are each slightly thicker and more sturdy than the previous one.

Again, the willow or hedgerow border would be better pricked-down at about $\frac{3}{8}$ in above the border; for the beginner, all the way round, and even for the more experienced, at least the first 5 or 6 stakes.

In cane, nip the stakes if there is any hint of cracking. Do not nip or prick-down too close to the border—allow plenty of room for another stake to pass between the one turned down and the siding.

3-Rod Border

1. Starting at any stake, which we will call No. 1 and the next stakes 2, 3, 4, 5 and so on, turn down No. 1 behind 2 and back to the front to lie in front of No. 3.

2. Turn down No. 2 behind No. 3 and back to the front to lie in front of No. 4.

3. Turn down No. 3 behind No. 4 and back to the front to lie in front of No. 5. (Figure 50.)

4. Go back to the first stake and pass it in front of No. 4 and behind 5 and out to the front again. Now turn down stake No. 4 so that it lies side by side, but behind the first stake. (Figure 51.)

5. Now take stake No. 2 and pass it in front of No. 5 and behind 6 and to the front again and turn down the next upright stake No. 5, so that it lies side by side and behind No. 2.

6. Repeat with No. 3. There are now 3 pairs of canes at the front (Figure 52.)

7. Take the right hand one of the left pair, or count the 5th one from the right, and pass it in front of the next upright stake (No. 7) and behind the next, and out to the front again. Turn down No. 7 to lie beside and behind it. Once again there are 3 pairs of stakes out to the front.

8. Continue thus all the way round, remembering to take the 5th from the right each time, until there is only one upright stake left. To help yourself, once the beginning is down say the words '5th stake from the right goes in front of one and behind one, and the upright goes behind it', out loud, and *do* what you are saying.

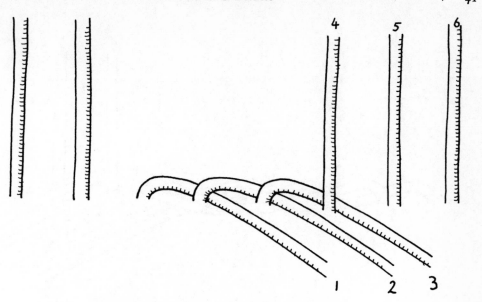

FIGURE 50. STARTING THE 3-ROD BORDER (1)

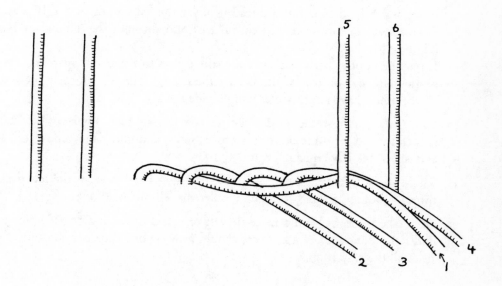

FIGURE 51. STARTING THE 3-ROD BORDER (2)

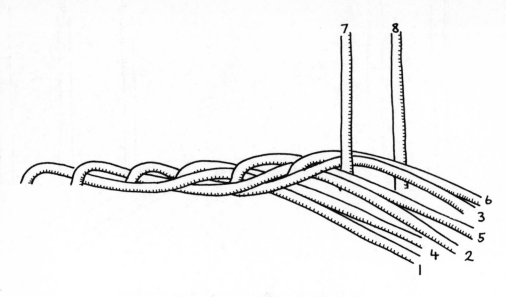

FIGURE 52. STARTING THE 3-ROD BORDER (3)

9. *To finish*; using the 5th stake from the right, pass it in front of the last upright stake, and behind No. 1 and thread it under the 'elbow' of No. 1. (Figure 53.) Turn down the last stake and thread that also through the 'elbow' of No. 1. (Figure 54.)
It may be noticed here that there are still 3 pairs to the front, apart from many single ones, and on top of the border there are 3 'elbows' on their own, while all the others have another one lying beside it.

10. *Cane Only.* To finish the border in cane, take the right hand stake of the left pair (as before) and thread it along side the 1st stake, and under the 'elbow' of No. 2 and out to the front again. (Figure 55.)

11. There are now only 2 pairs. Still take the right hand cane of the left pair and thread it alongside stake No. 2 and under the 'elbow' of No. 3.

12. Now take the right hand cane of the last pair, and thread it alongside No. 3 and under the 'elbow' of No. 4. There should now be one cane coming out of each space all the way round.

Make sure that the last 3 canes came to the front at the bottom of the border as all the others did.

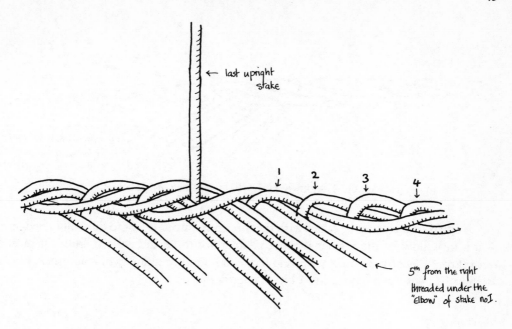

← last upright
stake

1 2 3 4

← 5th from the right
threaded under the
"elbow" of stake no I.

FIGURE 53. FINISHING THE 3-ROD BORDER IN CANE (1)

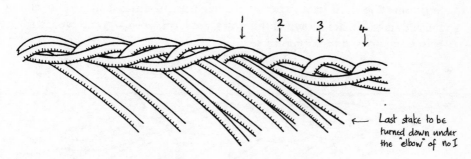

1 2 3 4

← Last stake to be
turned down under
the "elbow" of no I

FIGURE 54. FINISHING THE 3-ROD BORDER IN CANE (2)

The stakes may be trimmed close at this stage or left long to continue with a follow-on
or back-trac border.

To Finish the 3-Rod Border in Willow

The 3-rod border can be finished in willow or hedgerow, as it is for cane, but usually
only when a follow-on or back trac border is required.

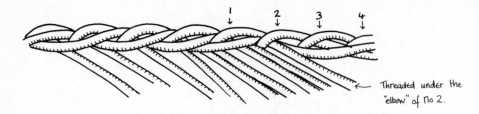

FIGURE 55. FINISHING THE 3-ROD BORDER IN CANE (3)

Very great care must be taken with the threading through (not so difficult in hedgerow as it is in willow, as the former is more pliable) not to let the willow 'kink'. It must be *eased* through gently pushing with one hand and gently pulling with the other. Do not attempt this until you have quite a bit of willow practice.

To Cram Off

The usual ending to a rod border in willow is to cram off. Follow the instructions up to No. 10, taking great care with the threading under the first 'elbow'.

10. Still using the right hand stake of the left pair, measure it up to the 'elbow' of the 2nd stake. Prick it down at this point, cut it off, with a good slype, 2 in or 3 in below the prick-down. (Figure 56).

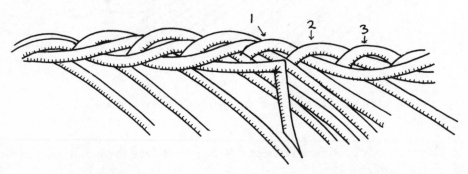

FIGURE 56. CRAMMING OFF THE 3-ROD BORDER IN WILLOW (1)

11. Slip this end down beside the left side of the 2nd stake. Use the bodkin to help you and rap down, very gently, with the iron. (Figure 57.)

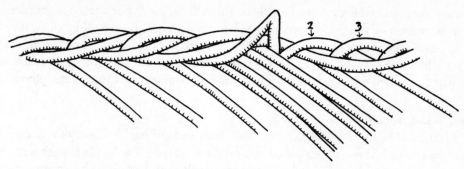

FIGURE 57. CRAMMING OFF THE 3-ROD BORDER IN WILLOW (2)

12. Now there are 2 pairs left. Once again take the right hand stake of the left pair and measure it up to the 'elbow' of the 3rd stake, and continue as before.

13. Repeat with the last right hand stake, measuring up to the 'elbow' of the 4th stake. Although I have said measure 'to the elbow' each time, to make the explanation easier, in actual fact, the measurement should be to the space before the stake, that is a little shorter than to the stake.

14. Pick-off the remainder of the stakes.

2-Rod, 4-Rod & 6-Rod Borders

These are all put on in exactly the same way as the 3-rod. In each case to start the border, turn down the *number* of stakes (behind the next stake to it on the right) as the *number* of the rod border. In other words, if it is to be a 2-rod border then turn down 2 stakes to begin with and if it is to be a 6-rod border, then turn down 6 stakes to begin with.

When beginning the larger rod borders (4, 5 and 6) do not turn down the first stakes too tightly, but leave a little loop before passing behind the next stake, so that there is room for the finishing stakes to fit in with them. Otherwise the border will look thin and tight at this point.

To continue the border always use the right hand stake of the most left hand pair. If you prefer to count the stakes the following table will help you.

3rd stake from the right for a 2-Rod border
5th stake from the right for a 3-Rod border
7th stake from the right for a 4-Rod border
9th stake from the right for a 5-Rod border
11th stake from the right for a 6-Rod border

As before pass this stake in front of the next upright stake and behind the next, and return it to the front, and then turn down the next upright stake to lie beside but behind it.

Finish exactly as for the 3-rod border, except that with the 2-rod only the first 2 strokes from 10 (cramming off or threading through) will be used. For the 4-rod border, after the three strokes of the 3-rod border have been completed, there will be one more pair, and so again take the right hand one of that pair and measure it up to or thread it under the 5th 'elbow'. Similarly, with a 5 or 6-rod border, continue until the right hand one of each pair has either been crammed off or threaded through the appropriate 'elbow'.

Behind 2-Rod Borders

All the rod borders described so far have been 'behind one' borders, that is, each time a stake was turned down, it was passed behind the next ONE. If a thicker border is required, then turn each stake down behind the next TWO stakes, and continue by passing the right one of the most left hand pair, in front of one and behind TWO.

PLAIT BORDERS

This very attractive border is no more difficult to do in cane than any of the others, but it is more difficult to learn how to start and finish it. Do not be discouraged if you have to be shown, or have the book in front of you for many attempts.

In willow it is more difficult to keep the stuff even and free from kinks—but practice makes perfect. Remember at all times to keep the stakes quite upright until they are turned down to use.

You will find it easier if you nip the stakes of anything thicker than No. 6 cane about $\frac{1}{4}$ in above the siding. (Do so if there is any tendency for the stakes to crack.) Nip so that the stakes will turn down sideways and nip all the way round before you start the border. For willow and hedgerow, prick-down before you start.

Commencing the Plait

Cut 2 small pieces of cane 2 in long, and 3 longer pieces; the same length as the remaining amount of stake for caneworkers and about 12 in for willow workers. All these extra pieces should be the same thickness as the stakes. The short pieces are merely 'cushions' over which to turn down the first stakes so that they are not too close to the siding. The long ones are substitutes for the 3 stakes immediately before the place where you start. At the finish (for cane only) they will be removed and the real ones threaded through in their place. Don't worry if the 'cushions' fall out before you are right round—their job is over once the stake is turned down into place over them.

Start anywhere you like, except over the step up of the waling beneath, or near a handle liner.

    1. Place one of the 'cushions' against a stake, we will call it stake 1, on the right side of it, resting against the top of the waling and at right angles to that waling.

2. Turn that stake down over the 'cushion', sideways to the right but in front of the other stakes.

3. Then place one of the substitute stakes beside it and to the right of it, with a few inches projecting to the inside of the basket. (Figure 58.)

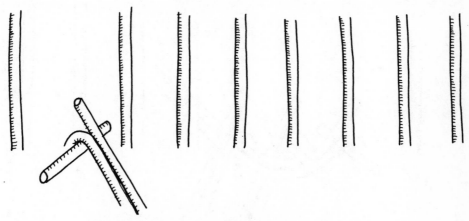

FIGURE 58. STARTING THE PLAIT BORDER (1)

4. Repeat 1, 2 and 3 with the second stake. There are now 2 pairs of rods to the front. (Figure 59.)

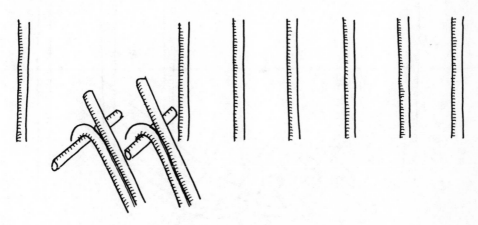

FIGURE 59. STARTING THE PLAIT BORDER (2)

5. Take the left hand pair into the centre of the basket, in between the next 2 upright stakes (not too tightly—allow a little loop to match up with all the others later).

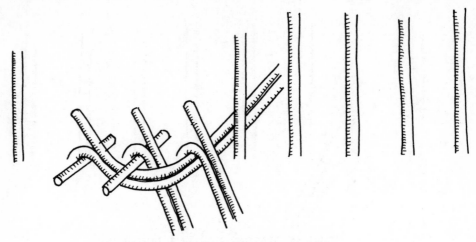

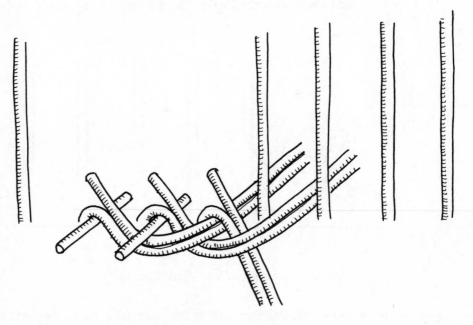

6. Turn down stake 3 over them, to the right but in front of the remaining upright ones.

7. Place the third substitute stake beside it and behind it as before. (Figure 60.)

8. Once again take the left hand pair of rods into the centre (Figure 61) between the

FIGURE 60. STARTING THE PLAIT BORDER (3)

FIGURE 61. STARTING THE PLAIT BORDER (4)

next 2 upright stakes and turn down stake 4 over them. You now have 2 pairs of stakes to the inside of the basket. (Figure 62.)

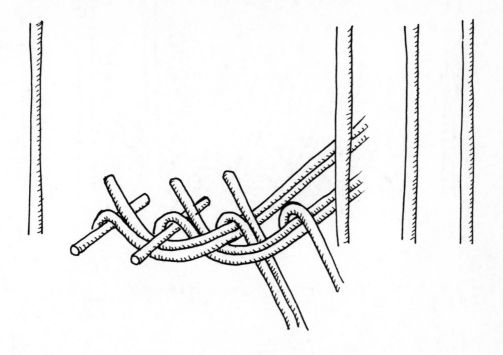

FIGURE 62. STARTING THE PLAIT BORDER (5)

9. Bring the left hand of the inside pairs back to the front. Behind (but lying quite flat) stake 4, that is the one you have just turned down. Now you have one pair to the left, and a group of 3 to the right, in front, and one pair on the inside. (Figure 63.)

10. Take the pair into the centre between the next 2 upright stakes (as before) and once again turn down the next stake No. 5 over it. Once again you have 2 pairs of stakes on the inside of the basket.

11. Bring the left hand pair back out to the front behind and beside No. 5. You now have 2 groups of 3 in the front. (Figure 64.)

12. Now count the 5th and 6th from the right of these stakes (they're the last this time, but they wont be the last next time so *count carefully*) and pass these to the inside, turn the next upright No. 6 over them and bring the left hand of the 2 inside pairs back out to the front to lie behind and beside stake No. 6. (Figure 65.)

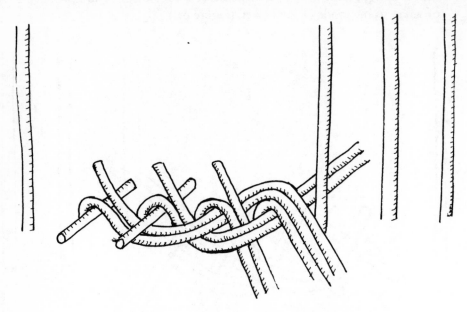

FIGURE 63. STARTING THE PLAIT BORDER (6)

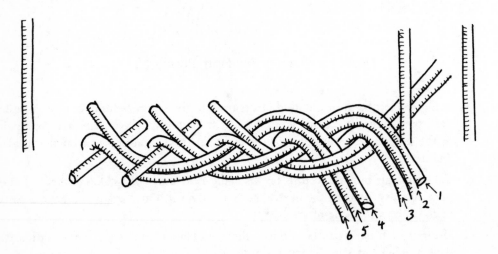

FIGURE 64. STARTING THE PLAIT BORDER (7)

Now continue with the border saying to yourself, '5 and 6 go in, upright down, and the left hand pair comes out', for every single stroke, and do what you say.

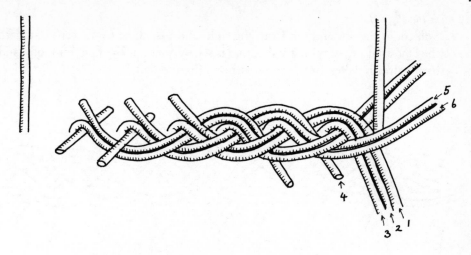

FIGURE 65. STARTING THE PLAIT BORDER (8)

If you suddenly find that you have a short one and it wont reach to the end of the stroke, you have done one of two things (that is, providing the stakes all started off the same length):

(a) You have counted wrongly and the ones you passed to the middle were *not* the 5th and the 6th from the right, or

(b) You twisted either 5 and 6, or the inside pair, as you passed them through.
If you have a tendency to twist either of these over, pass them through one at a time (especially if the cane is thick) until you are more practised.

Be very careful to turn the stakes down so that there is no gap between the siding and the border. Check every so often!

Continue with '5 and 6 in, upright down and the left hand pair out', until you are right round the border and NO stakes are left upright. (Figure 66.)

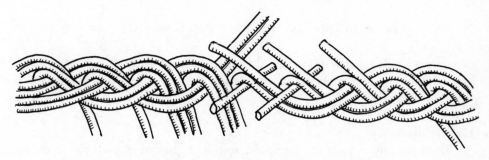

FIGURE 66. FINISHING THE PLAIT BORDER IN CANE (1)

To Finish the Plait Border

1. Still count the 5th and 6th from the right and pass these to the centre underneath the elbow of the very first stake, that is where you put the first 'cushion', and if it hasn't already fallen out, remove it now. (Figure 67.)

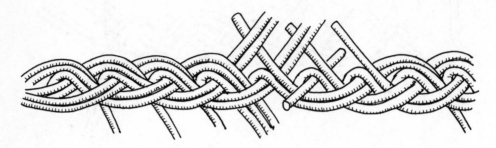

FIGURE 67. FINISHING THE PLAIT BORDER IN CANE (2)

2. Take the 2nd and 3rd from the right and take these to the inside underneath the 'elbow' of the 2nd stake (where you put the 2nd cushion, and remove that now). (Figure 68.)

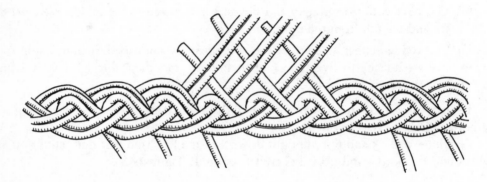

FIGURE 68. FINISHING THE PLAIT BORDER IN CANE (3)

If you are plaiting with willow, do these last 2 movements with great care to avoid 'kinking' the willow in the wrong places. Push gently as well as pull gently and try to keep the willow ROUND.

For Cane Workers only

3. There are now 3 pairs on the inside, and the right one of each pair is the longer. (The 3 ends of the substitute canes are also protruding into the centre at this same

point). Each of these 3 longer canes will replace a substitute one, keeping in the correct order, as they are now, of left, middle, right.

4. Start with the left one and gradually remove the substitute cane and put in the true one—stroke by stroke; using the bodkin, and by pointing the ends of the canes to help you. Never take so much of the substitute cane out, that you have *lost* the place for the real one to go. Finally the substitute cane will come right away and the real one is protruding to the front like all the other stakes. (Figures 69 and 70.)

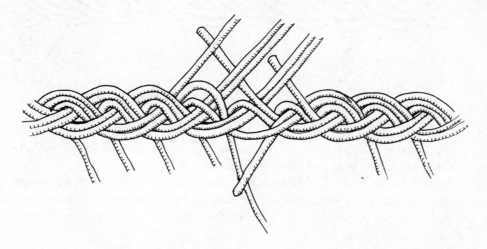

FIGURE 69. FINISHING THE PLAIT BORDER IN CANE (4)

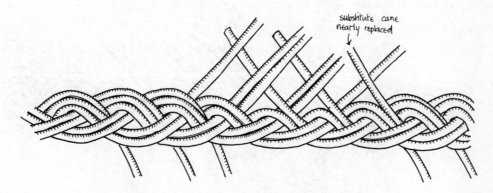

FIGURE 70. FINISHING THE PLAIT BORDER IN CANE (5)

5. Now replace the middle and right hand stakes. (Figure 71.) At this stage you will have just 3 separate canes protruding into the centre. Thread each of these 3 remaining inside stakes, 'one plait' to the right so that they return to the front in the same way and position as all the other stakes.

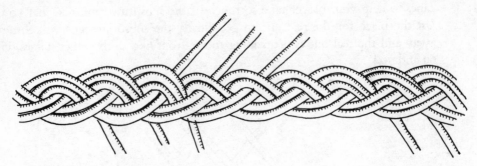

FIGURE 71. FINISHING THE PLAIT BORDER IN CANE (6)

For Willow & Hedgerow Workers

3. Do not attempt to remove the substitute rods in willow and hedgerow but leave them permanently in and finish instead like this:
   As in the cane border at this stage, there are 3 pairs to the inside of the basket, and the 3 ends of the substitute rods. Take each of the 3 substitute ends in turn and tuck each one into the border one 'plait' to the LEFT, so that it comes back out to the front again. (Figure 72.)

4. Now take the right hand one of each of the 3 pairs on the inside, and tuck it inside and through the border one plait to the RIGHT round the outside of the substitute rods that you have just used. This will make up the correct number of rods to the plait. (Figure 73.)

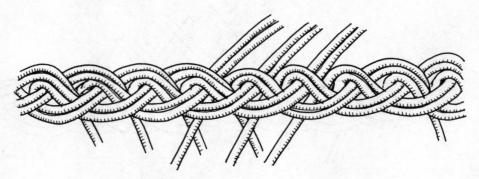

FIGURE 72. FINISHING THE PLAIT BORDER IN WILLOW (1)

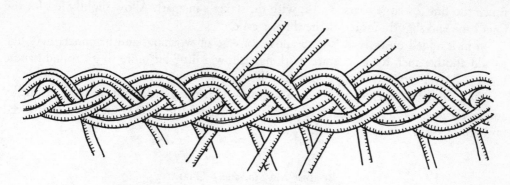

FIGURE 73. FINISHING THE PLAIT BORDER IN WILLOW (2)

Try to keep all this very flat and 'unkinked': although it sounds simpler than the cane finish, it does require practice to make it smooth and even.

Pick off all the ends as close as possible.

FOLLOW-ON, BACK-TRAC & OTHER BORDERS

Any 2 of these borders can be used together, using one on the top of the siding and a 2nd put on at the side of the first border. It could be a plait put on after a 3-rod border, with the plait coming in front of the 3-rod; or a 3-rod coming after a 3 or 4-rod border. This makes a particularly thick and attractive border and is excellent for willow and hedgerow. It is one of my favourite borders. Or you could have, say, a trac No. 2, after a larger trac.

By finishing a trac border on the inside of the basket, and putting on a follow-on simple trac, you can make a ridge to support a lid.

A flower basket would look attractive with a series of, say 7 or 8 rounds of trac No. 1.

A 3 or 4-rod border in cane is neatened by using trac borders No. 1 or 2 and passing the ends through the basket, between the border and the siding, to lie on the inside, where they are trimmed off.

N.B. A follow-on border is a 2nd border put on after the first and travelling in the same direction as the first. A back-trac border is a 2nd border put on after the first but travelling in the opposite direction to the first.

You will say to yourself, 'But how much cane, or willow do I allow for these borders?' So I have made out a chart to give you a guide—page 56.

Explanation of the Border Measurement Chart

I have used No. 8 cane in working out this chart, for the sake of uniformity, although this would be much too thick for miniature work, with the stakes only $\frac{1}{4}$ in apart, and much too fine for large coarse work, with the stakes 2 in apart. Allow slightly less for the finer cane and slightly more for the thicker cane.

   I in is added on in each case to allow for ease of working, and beginners may like to add another inch for inaccurate working. Allow a little bit more to go round handle liners and over raised work, e.g. tray handles.

   The amount required for a follow-on or a back-trac border can be worked out by adding the lengths of the 2 borders required, together, less I in. You wont need I in allowed on both of them 'for ease of working'.

BORDER MEASUREMENT CHART
To show length of cane or willow to allow for each type of border

Distance between Stakes★	$\frac{1}{4}$ in	$\frac{1}{2}$ in	$\frac{3}{4}$ in	I in	$1\frac{1}{4}$ in	$1\frac{1}{2}$ in	2 in
	in	in	in	in	in	in	in
TRAC NO. I	$1\frac{3}{4}$	$2\frac{1}{4}$	$2\frac{3}{4}$	$3\frac{1}{4}$	$3\frac{3}{4}$	$4\frac{1}{4}$	$5\frac{1}{4}$
TRAC NO. 2	2	$2\frac{3}{4}$	$3\frac{1}{2}$	$4\frac{1}{4}$	5	$5\frac{3}{4}$	$7\frac{1}{4}$
TRAC NO. 3	$2\frac{1}{4}$	$3\frac{1}{4}$	$4\frac{1}{4}$	$5\frac{1}{4}$	$6\frac{1}{4}$	$7\frac{1}{4}$	$9\frac{1}{4}$
TRAC NO. 4	$2\frac{1}{2}$	$3\frac{3}{4}$	$5\frac{1}{4}$	$6\frac{1}{2}$	$7\frac{1}{4}$	9	$10\frac{1}{4}$
TRAC NO. 5	$3\frac{1}{4}$	$4\frac{1}{2}$	$5\frac{3}{4}$	7	$8\frac{1}{4}$	$9\frac{1}{2}$	12
TRAC NO. 6	$4\frac{3}{4}$	7	$9\frac{1}{4}$	$11\frac{1}{2}$	$13\frac{3}{4}$	16	$20\frac{1}{2}$
3-ROD	$3\frac{1}{2}$	5	$6\frac{1}{2}$	8	$9\frac{1}{2}$	11	14
4-ROD	$3\frac{3}{4}$	$5\frac{1}{2}$	$7\frac{1}{4}$	9	$10\frac{3}{4}$	$12\frac{1}{2}$	16
5-ROD	4	6	8	10	12	14	18
6-ROD	$4\frac{1}{4}$	$6\frac{1}{2}$	$8\frac{3}{4}$	11	$13\frac{1}{4}$	$15\frac{1}{2}$	20
PLAIT	$4\frac{1}{4}$	6	$7\frac{3}{4}$	$9\frac{1}{2}$	$11\frac{1}{4}$	13	$16\frac{1}{2}$

★ Measured from the *centre* of one stake to the *centre* of the next.

5. *Handles, Fastenings & Hinges*

HANDLES

There are various ways of putting on a handle. The handle must be compatible with the basket. Do not put a thin weedy handle on a shopping basket or it will cut into your hands, but a thick handle on a wine basket would look clumsy and ungainly. Handles come, roughly into 2 categories: (1) Cross handles, and (2) Small handles.

Cross Handles

This handle goes across the basket (either the width or the length) and requires a handle bow, which is inserted right down into the siding beside a stake. In order to get this deep insertion, a space has to be kept open during the weaving, by putting in *handle liners* next to the stake (the space is called a bow-mark) where the handle will eventually go.

The handle liner is made from a piece of handle cane, or thick willow or even a piece of stick, as long as it is the same thickness, or slightly smaller than the handle bow itself. (Otherwise the space made would be too big and wouldn't grip the handle sufficiently well.) The liners would need to be about 5 in or 6 in for a small basket and 8 in to 9 in for a large one, and have a large slype (see page 5) at one end.

Have twice as many handle liners as handle bows that you are putting in, i.e. if your basket is to have 3 bows (as the basket on page 141) then you will have 6 liners, one for each end of each bow. Insert them as in Figure 74.

Weave round them as if they were joined to the stake, and weave round them for the border, making the strokes of the border go round them in whichever way the border looks neatest.

Make sure that at least 3 in of the liner protrudes from the basket after the border is down or you will find them very difficult to remove. If the siding of the basket has grown higher than you intended and the liners are getting short, keep lifting them up as you go.

When the border is finished and the handle bows are ready, remove the liners but do not discard them—they will do for very many baskets yet.

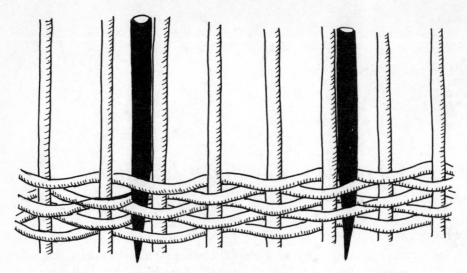

FIGURE 74. INSERTING THE HANDLE LINERS

The handle bow itself (or bows) is measured, cut, shaped and slyped and inserted into the bow-marks—the spaces made by the handle liners. For a cane basket, 8 or 10 mm handle cane, or glossy handle cane is used. For willow or hedgerow, use either a piece of stout willow, or an ash or a hazel stick.

When measuring the required length, remember that the bow should go further into the siding than the liners, in fact as near to the base as possible.

Shape the willow, ash, or hazel gradually and carefully and tie it into shape for an hour or so, before slyping and using.

If a rope handle (Plate 18) is required, only one handle bow is put in, but if the handle is to be wrapped it may have 1, 2 or 3 bows, which are inserted into the basket singly and then joined by nails or sellotape, or both, across the top of the handle. The middle one of the 3 bows may be thinner than the other 2. When using 2 or 3 bows the beginning and the end may be wrapped separately or randed or left plain, until the bows join together when they are wrapped as one.

The Rope Handle

This handle is used much more often than a wrapped one for willow and hedgerow and less often for cane. It makes a lovely sturdy handle using only one bow.

1. Select 8 or 10 long fine rods of willow, or whatever hedgerow stuff is being used, making quite sure that there are no blemishes or kinks, or cut the same number of lengths of No. 4 or 5 cane (thinner of course for small or miniature work) to go over the handle plus 15 in.

2. Slype one end of each rod or cane (the butt end for willow or hedegrow) and insert 4 into the siding to the left of one end of the handle bow, in such a way that they are not in a bunch, but in a row round the bow.

3. Repeat at the other end. Reserve the remaining 2 for the moment.

4. Starting with one set of 4 rods, wrap them anticlockwise (so that they come in front of the bow first) 3 or 4 times, evenly over the bow to the other side, and leave the ends for the moment, lying inside the basket. (Figure 75.)

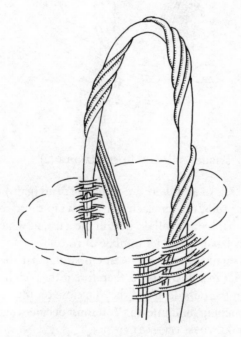

FIGURE 75. THE ROPE HANDLE (1)

5. Now take the other 4 rods and do exactly the same, fitting these into the spaces made by the first 4, and leave them for the moment, inside the basket. (Figure 76.)

Very great care must be taken not to 'kink' the willow and hedgerow rods (if any do they must be replaced) and both hands must be used to help the rods through, with the tips leading the way. The basket should be firmly anchored with weights or board while you are doing this so that both hands are free. You may find it easier to put all the rods through together so that they support each other, or you may find it easier to put them through singly. I prefer the former method but I advise you to experiment for yourself.

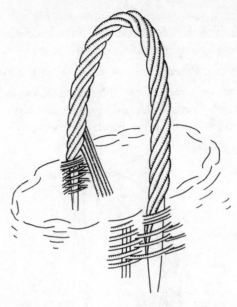

FIGURE 76. THE ROPE HANDLE (2)

Having put over both sets of 4, if there are any large grins (gaps) in the weaving show-ing, add in the 2 remaining rods, one on each side and wrap those round in the same way to fill the gaps. (It may be that these 2 still do not fill the gaps, in which case add in 2 more. Always see that the 2 sides have the same number of rods.)

If the grins are only small, leave them—remembering that the measurement of the inside of the handle is smaller than the outside, therefore if the rods lie closely on the inside, there will be slight gaps on the outside and if they lie close on the outside, the chances are that there will be some 'bunching' underneath. You must decide which you like best—only an expert (or luck) CAN MAKE THEM PERFECTLY EVEN.

However, if they are very uneven, don't be afraid to take them all out and start from the beginning again. You may resoak cane, but discard willow or hedgerow rods and select new ones.

To Finish the Rope Handle

1. Pass all the rods at one end from the inside of the basket to the outside, through or under the waling, and at the right side of the bow. (Looking at the outside of the basket.)

2. Take them diagonally up across the waling to the left side of the bow.

3. Take them round the back of the bow and then diagonally down across and in front of the waling.

4. Pass them back to the inside of the basket, again through the waling, this time on the left of the bow, taking care to go under the same round of waling each time (and on both sides of the basket) and to keep the rods in the correct order all the time. (Figure 77.)

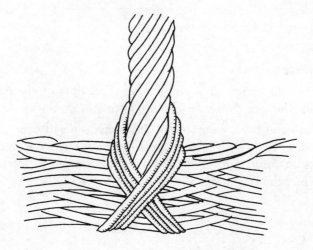

FIGURE 77. FINISHING THE ROPE HANDLE

5. Weave the ends away securely, i.e. to pass them in and out of the siding some to the right and some to the left.

6. Repeat at the other end.

An Alternative Ending

1. As before pass the ends from the inside to the outside of the basket through the waling and diagonally up and across the waling to the left side of the handle bow.

2. Take them round to the back of the bow, but this time leave them standing upright.

3. Using one of the rods, wrap round and round the handle and the other rods.

4. Finally tuck the tip of this rod through the wrapping and pull tight.

5. Secure with a small nail and trim all the ends.

All basket makers have their own favourite way of finishing a rope handle and there are many other ways beside these two. My favourite is the first but you must try them and decide for yourself.

A Wrapped Handle, using a Single Bow

Glossy wrapping cane, flat cane, chair seating cane or a skein from a willow or hedge-row rod (see page 8) can be used. A leader is nearly always used, as it keeps the wrapping tight as well as adding a little decoration. A leader is a rod or skein which goes across the basket and is wrapped over and under by the wrapping cane. More than one leader can be used at once and many interesting patterns can be made (Plate 3). The leader can be made from the same stuff as the wrapping, or it can be a whole cane or rod or enamelled cane if colour is desired. The leader need only be the same length as the handle to be wrapped, plus 1 in or 2 in for ease of working.

Commencing the Wrapped Handle

1. Insert the cane (or skein) through or under the waling on the right side of handle bow, so that the cane protrudes about 6 in or 7 in on the inside of the basket.
2. Pull the short end from the inside of the basket, up and over the border, still on the right side of the bow. Take it diagonally down across the outside of the waling, and once again thread it through the waling, this time on the left of the handle bow, and up to lie behind or inside the bow. (Figure 78.)

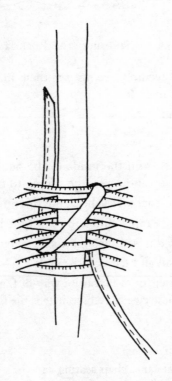

FIGURE 78. THE WRAPPED HANDLE (1)

3. Now take the *other* end diagonally up and across the waling to the left of the handle bow, and wrap 3 times round the handle bow *and* the short end of the wrapping cane. (Figure 79.)

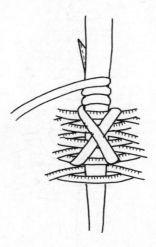

FIGURE 79. THE WRAPPED HANDLE (2)

4. Insert the leader into these first rounds of the wrapping, on the outside of the bow.

5. Continue wrapping but pass the wrapping cane alternately over and under the leader, at the same time binding in the short end until it is quite secure, when any surplus may be cut off. (Figure 80.)

To Finish the Wrapping

1. When the other end is reached, cut off any surplus leader, so that it lies flat and wrap the final 3 rounds plain, to match the beginning. (The beginning and end is always wrapped plain—the number of rounds varying, partly according to the size of the basket and wrapping cane, and partly to personal choice. However both ends should be the same, although this is not always possible with the more complicated leader patterns.)

2. Finish with a cross to match the beginning, making sure that the cane is passed under the same round of waling as the beginning.

3. Weave the end away by passing it in and out, directly underneath the border.

To Join In when Wrapping

1. Insert the new piece of cane or skein, into the back, or inside, of the handle, with

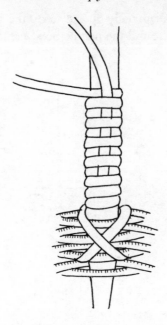

FIGURE 80. THE WRAPPED HANDLE (3)

the wrong side of the cane outwards, when there is about 12 in of the old piece left (or enough to do another 1½ in–2 in of lapping).

2. Continue to wrap with the old cane, keeping any patterns correct and the new piece bound in at the back, until there is only 1½ in–2 in of the old cane left. (Figure 81A.)

3. Turn the new piece at an angle of 45°, away from the old piece.

4. Turn the old end at an angle of 45° at the back of the handle, so that it lies against the handle with the wrong side uppermost. (Figure 81B.)

5. Continue wrapping with the new piece, at the same time binding the old piece in at the back. Keep all the binding very tight during this process. (Figure 81C.)

Pegging the Handles

The single cross of the wrapping skein is not sufficient to keep the handle in place during use, and we must PEG the handle, if we do not wish it to slip out of its sockets.

With the handle cane sufficiently damped, pierce a hole in between the waling and into the bow, using the bodkin.

Make a peg of number 10 or 12 cane, about 1 in long and well pointed at one end.

Push the peg into the hole made by the bodkin, using the iron or hammer to knock into position if necessary, until the peg is flush with the waling on the outside of the basket.

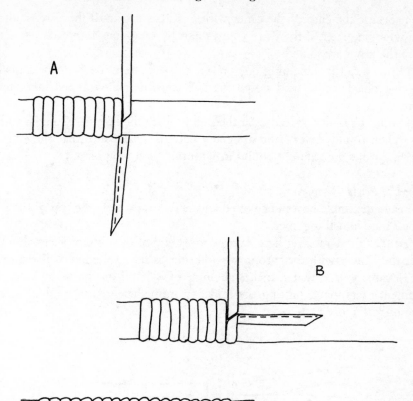

FIGURE 81. JOINING-IN WHEN WRAPPING A HANDLE

Clip any surplus on the inside so that the peg is lying flush with the waling on the inside of the basket.

If later on, this peg slips out, secure with a little glue, when it is quite dry.

To Wrap a Handle with 2 or 3 Bows

When inserting the bows into the siding, make sure that they are both or all, *exactly* the same height, or the handle will be lopsided and difficult to work. Join them securely together across the top with nails and/or sellotape. There are 3 ways of wrapping this type of handle.

Method 1, All Wrapped (Plate 11)

If there are 2 bows, start by wrapping *one* on each side, up to the point where the handle bows join. Start in exactly the same way as for the single bow, but do not use a leader. Secure the ends of the canes with a clothes peg until they are bound in with the main wrapping later. If there are 3 bows start by wrapping 2 on each side up to the point where the bows are joined.

Now wrap the remaining one on one side and continue with the same piece of cane over the joined section and down the last remaining unwrapped bow, to finish off as before.

Join in the leader or leaders at the point where the bows are joined, and as before do a few plain rounds before and after any pattern. Make sure that the ends of the other wrapping canes are securely bound in with the main wrapping.

Method 2, *Partly Wrapped*

Leave the single bows uncovered and only wrap across the top of the handle, where the bows are joined together.

To start the wrapping here, lay the short end of the cane or skein about 2 in or 3 in, under the handle with the wrong side outside, as far to the left as is required. Turn the cane towards you so that it makes an angle of 45° still on the under side of the handle. Commence wrapping, putting the leader in immediately, and binding in the short end at the back. (Figure 82.)

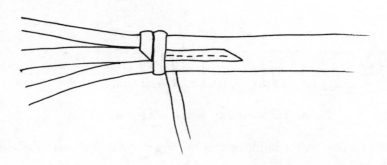

FIGURE 82. STARTING THE PARTLY WRAPPED HANDLE

Finish by threading the end under the last few rounds, wrong side to the outside, so that it makes the same neat angle as at the beginning, pull tight and trim. A small nail can be used at the beginning and the end for extra security. (Figure 83.)

Method 3, *Rand and Wrap*

Insert a slyped butt or piece of cane into the border beside one of the handle bows and rand backwards and forwards up the handle until the bows meet. (Figure 84.) Repeat on the other side. Finish the handle as for Method 2.

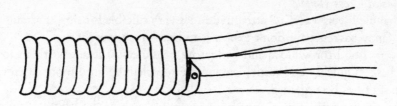

FIGURE 83. THE PARTLY WRAPPED HANDLE

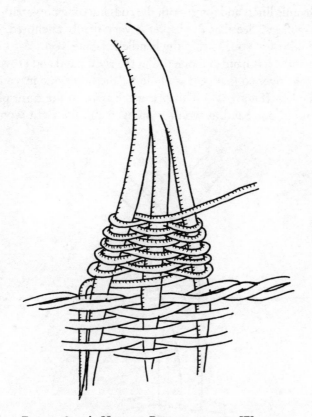

FIGURE 84. A HANDLE RANDED BEFORE WRAPPING

Keep the weavers very fine for this handle, and choose "kind" rods. Arrange the piecing in so that you finish with a tip which is bound in by the wrapping. Put the randing on slowly and carefully, especially when using willow or hedgerow stuffs, helping the rods through with both hands (the basket will still be anchored firmly by weights or board). Keep the randing as close and tight as possible or it will be loose when it dries out.

Simple Twisted Cross Handle

This handle is very easy and attractive and is very suitable for flower arranging baskets and small fancy baskets. But don't expect it to bear much weight.

It is very good for willow and hedgerow beginners as it allows them to complete their first baskets quickly and easily, leaving the rope handle until more experience in the feel of the stuff has been gained.

Cut and slype both ends of 2 rods, or pieces of cane, to the length required, that is, over the basket and well down into the siding on both sides. Choose fairly stout rods, and about No. 15 cane.

Remove the handle liners and insert both the rods into one bow mark, as far down into the siding as they will go. See that the basket is very firmly anchored, or better still get someone else to hold it for you, so that the handle is facing you.

Take one rod in the left hand and one rod in the right hand and cross your hands over. Now change the rods over so that you are holding the other one in your right hand and vice versa, with the left. (Figure 85.) This places the twist in the right place—do not just twist the rods round in one hand, it won't be as even and the twist won't be tight.

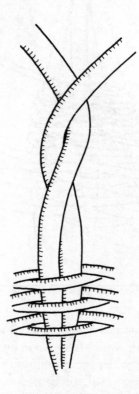

FIGURE 85. A SIMPLE TWISTED ROD HANDLE

Repeat this action, always crossing the same hand over the top of the other, until you have reached to within 3 in or 4 in of the end.

Insert these ends together into the bow mark on the opposite side of the basket.

Secure very firmly by knocking a small nail through a cane of the waling and into the handle bow on each side.

This handle can be put on using 4 or even 6 rods instead of just 2. After inserting them all into the same bow mark, take 2 or 3 in each hand and work as before, keeping the twists flat. (Figure 86.) This makes a very pretty handle for a flower basket.

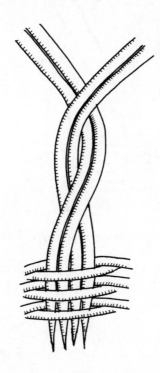

FIGURE 86. TWISTED HANDLE USING FOUR RODS

Another variation is for 4 bow marks to be made, 2 on each side of the basket, and 1 or 2 rods to be inserted in both the bow marks on one side. (Figure 87.)

Bring these 2 rods, or sets of rods, together for twisting after about 3 in or 4 in, and part them again 3 in or 4 in before the other side. Put 1 rod in each bow mark on the opposite side of the basket.

SMALL HANDLES
There is a great variety of small handles and these can be roped or wrapped as before. A small handle can be put on the side of a basket, after the border has been laid down;

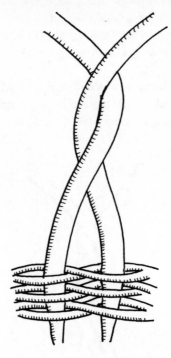

FIGURE 87. VARIATION OF THE SIMPLE TWISTED HANDLE

some are made quite separately and attached to the basket afterwards. Some are very simple and some require quite a lot of patience. However on the following pages you will find instructions for 4 or 5 of these small handles.

1. *Side Handles for an Oval Shopping Basket*

These are made in exactly the same way as the cross handle and can be either roped or wrapped.

Put handle liners in, half way up the siding to form bow marks. You will require 2 on each side of the basket. Make sure that they are wide enough apart to make the handle comfortable for the width of your hand. (Nothing is more tiring than a heavy basket with the handle too small—and you may want the menfolk to carry it one day. So allow for their hands, or they will have too good an excuse not to carry it.)

Shape, insert, wrap or rope, and peg each handle in exactly the same way as for the wrapped or roped handle with a single bow.

You will find that when both the handles are completed, they stand stiffly erect from the siding and that when you grip them together the sides of the basket come together also. This again makes the hands ache when carrying shopping and the basket is so full that the sides won't come together. To avoid this, soak the handles well and tie them to-gether at the top, and at the same time, place some books or a block of wood between the sides of the basket at border level to keep them in their right position. Wait at least a day for the handles to dry in this shape—it will be much more comfortable to use. (Figure 88.)

FIGURE 88. SHAPING THE HANDLES OF A SHOPPING BASKET

This same handle can be used at the sides of a roll or baby basket and would then be made smaller and daintier, perhaps using No. 15 cane instead of handle cane, and No. 2 chair seating cane for wrapping.

2. *Single Rod Small Handle*

Select a rod or piece of cane, long enough to go 3 times over the handle plus a few inches for weaving away. Slype the butt of the rod, insert it into the border at the point where you wish the left side of the border to be (no marks are necessary for this handle).

Take the rod across to the right side of the handle and thread it from the outside to the inside of the basket just underneath the border, forming a loop of the required size. (Figure 89.) The loose end of the rod is then taken 3 or 4 times round the loop back to the left side of the handle.

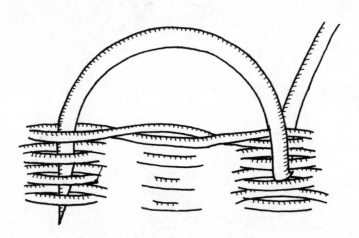

FIGURE 89. THE SINGLE ROD SMALL HANDLE (1)

There, once again it is threaded just under the border, from the outside to the inside of the basket. (Figure 90.)

Now take it back to the right side following the rope effect. (Figure 91.)

Pass the tip into the border and weave away. This handle should now look like a rope of 3 strands.

A Small Wrapped Handle Added Afterwards

This handle is made totally separately from the basket and is attached afterwards, with twisted or plaited loops. It can be of any size to suit the basket, and can be either round, oval or 'D' shaped.

Make the foundation first, of handle cane, well soaked and then tied into the required shape.

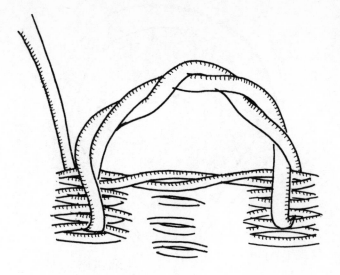

FIGURE 90. THE SINGLE ROD SMALL HANDLE (2)

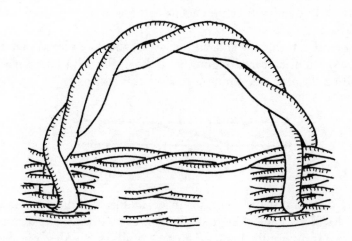

FIGURE 91. THE SINGLE ROD SMALL HANDLE (3)

To make a 'D' shape, nip hard with the round nosed pliers at the points where the curve ends. If the back of the 'D' still won't lie flat, cut a wedge shape out of the inside of the cane at this point. (Figure 92.)

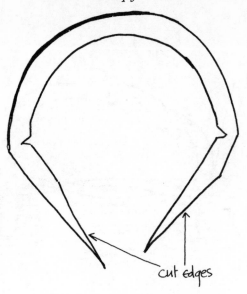

FIGURE 92. 'D' SHAPED HANDLE

Cut each of the ends (whatever the shape) so that they overlap by 2 in if possible. You may find it difficult to overlap much on a small ring, but on the other hand a large 'D' could overlap by 4 in or 5 in.

Make a diagonal cut on each end, so that when they are placed together these cuts make up the thickness of the cane. (Figures 93 and 94.) For a 'D' shape make this cut on the flat side, and on the long side for an oval shape. (Figure 95.)

FIGURE 93. DIAGONAL CUT

Tie all this firmly into shape, once it is made, and leave it until it is thoroughly dry. (I always think that it is a good thing to make 2 or even 3 handles at this stage, and then choose the one that turns out the best—or if they are all perfect, then put the unused ones away for future use.)

When it is dry, untie the string that is holding the cut and glue and nail the cut into position. Re-tie, and again leave it to dry thoroughly. (It is not possible to glue in the first place, because the glue will not stick on a wet surface. However if the handle is fairly large and the cut long and keeps in place easily, then just nailing and binding with thin fuse wire will be sufficient.)

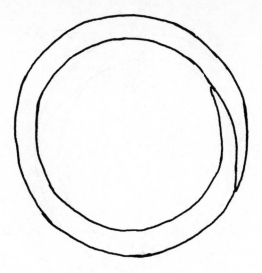

FIGURE 94. A SMALL RING SHOWING THE DIAGONAL JOIN

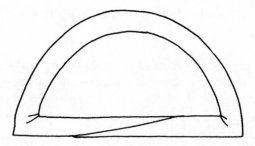

FIGURE 95. 'D'-SHAPED HANDLE SHOWING THE DIAGONAL JOIN

Untie and make quite sure that the handle is quite firm and sturdy. Don't attempt to start wrapping it until it is, and if necessary start from the beginning again. Smooth any rough edges with sand-paper.

To Wrap a Small Handle

1. Use a fine chair seating cane for the wrapping and use a leader, at least across the front.

2. Start the wrapping in exactly the same way as for the partly-wrapped Cross Handle (see page 66). For a ring start on the inside, and for an oval or a 'D' shape, start at the back of the work. (Figure 96.)

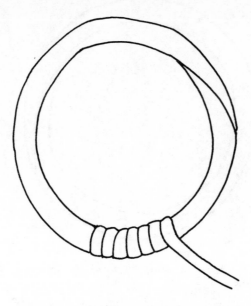

FIGURE 96. WRAPPING THE SMALL RING

3. Continue wrapping round the handle, remembering that the inside measurement
is less than the outside, on a curve, so the cane must overlap slightly on the insides
of the curve. The corners of the 'D' shape are rather tricky and the wrapping cane
will have to overlap quite a lot on the inside to keep the outside covered. The leader
passing over these corners will help so be sure to join it in just before the corner.
(Figure 97.)

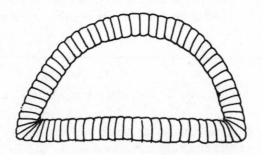

FIGURE 97. THE WRAPPED 'D' SHAPE

4. When the wrapping is complete, finish as for the partly wrapped handle making sure that the beginning and the end lie closely and neatly together. (Figure 83.)

To attach these handles, insert a piece of No. 6 or 8 cane, well soaked, into the weaving (preferably the waling) next to a stake, at the place where the handle is to go.

Take the cane round the back of the stake and out to the front again, through the same round of weaving as before. (Figure 98.)

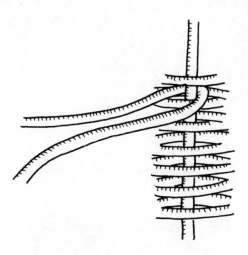

FIGURE 98. ATTACHING THE SMALL RING (1)

Twist the 2 ends together, by crossing over the hands and changing the canes over, as for the simple twisted handle on page 68 for the length required to make a loop. Thread the handle on and pass the 2 ends of the loop canes through the weaving, one on each side of the same stake as before, cross them over at the back of the stake and weave the ends away. (Figure 99.)

A 'D' or oval shape would require at least 2 loops, but a ring may only need one.

Do make sure that these loops are sturdy enough for the handle, the basket, and the job required. See that the handle is held firmly against the basket, but not so tight that it cannot rotate in the loops.

A plait may be used with 3 weavers, instead of a twist with only 2.

To attach a ring to a round lid, the same method may be used by inserting the cane round one or two of the sticks on one side of the cross and finishing round the same sticks on the other side of the cross. (Use the bodkin to help.)

An alternative method of attaching a ring is to bind over and over, with one piece of cane, which can be round or flat cane, or a willow skein passing into and round the back of the weaving and out and round the ring. Weave both the ends of this cane away. (Figure 100.)

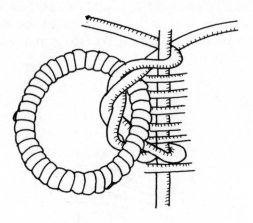

FIGURE 99. ATTACHING THE SMALL RING (2)

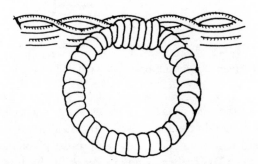

FIGURE 100. ALTERNATIVE METHOD OF ATTACHING THE SMALL HANDLE

A Simple Twisted Ring

This makes quite an attractive handle for the lid of a work basket, or to hang a bell, etc—see Plate 9. It is not very strong so don't use it to carry any weight.

You will need a piece of cane, 3 times the length of the circumference of the circle required, plus 2 in or 3 in for ease of working. Therefore for a 1 in ring, which has a circumference of approximately $3\frac{1}{4}$ in you will need to start with a cane of about 12 in to 13 in, and for a 2 in ring you will need 23 in.

Tie a piece of cane or willow, any thickness, in keeping with the basket, into a loop with a single knot and pull into the size required. (Figure 101.)

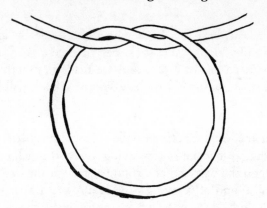

FIGURE 101. A SIMPLE TWISTED HANDLE

Take one end and twist it round and round the ring and so back to the knot.

Then take the other end, and again twist it round and round the ring the other way, following the twists of the first end, so that it looks like a 3 strand rope. (Figure 102.)

FIGURE 102. SIMPLE TWISTED HANDLE COMPLETED

Cut the ends away neatly at the same place and attach the ring in the same way as the previous handles.

A thicker ring can be made by following the twists round once or even twice more.

For other uses of this ring see the lampshades and the hanging flower basket in the pattern section. No doubt you can think of many more.

FASTENINGS

The best form of fastenings for the beginner are made by loops, which pass one over the other (a hasp and a loop), and a stick, peg or even a bead is used to secure them. They may be made with a twist or a plait and are made in exactly the same way as the loop for attaching the small wrapped handle, except that they will be larger.

The Loop

Position and make the loops first (for a willow basket it is better to put these on while you are doing the siding, as it makes the weaving away so much easier).

Insert a cane through the weaving and round a stake at the back and returning to the front through the same round of weaving—see Figure 98. Twist the 2 ends together by crossing over the hands with a cane in each hand, and transfer the canes in each hand to the other hand. Repeat for as many twists as are necessary, always passing the same hand over the top each time. (This is the only way that you can hope to make the twists really tight and even.)

Pass the 2 ends back into the work again, about ¾ in away from the start of the loop, round the back of the same stake, or through the same round of weaving if you are going sideways, and on to another stake, and weave the ends away. The loop should be just large enough for the stick or peg to fit tightly when the hasp is in position. (Figure 103.)

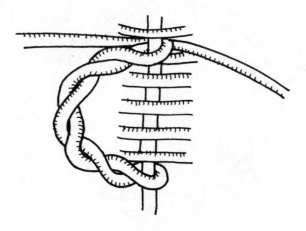

FIGURE 103. TWISTED LOOP FASTENING

The Hasp

The hasp, is made in the same way, starting and finishing by looping the cane or willow round either (*a*) the border, (*b*) a stake just inside the border, and the hasp will then go over the border and then turn down, or (*c*) the thick edge sticks in the case of a square lid.

The hasp may be made more elaborately by crossing over the twist half way down. This does ensure a more snug fit if the hasp needs to be rather long. Start as before and work until the twist is long enough to go right round the back to the top of the loop, then thread one of the canes through the twist at this point and continue and finish as before. (Figure 104.)

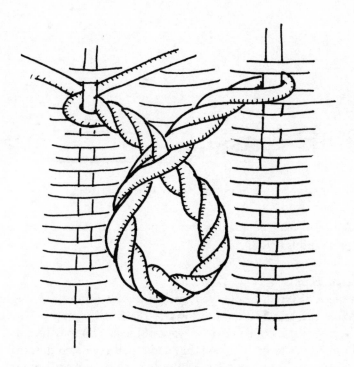

FIGURE 104. A MORE ELABORATE LOOP

All these hasps and loops can be made in exactly the same way with a plait instead of a twist, if you wish for a sturdier fastening.

The peg which goes through the loop, is generally made of handle cane, or a stick of similar size. It may be only a few inches long for a single fastening, or one long stick that will pass through 2 or more fastenings. The peg or stick should be attached to the basket by a very fine cane passing through a hole drilled fairly near the end of the peg, twisted for 4 in or 5 in and the ends woven away in the basket. Alternatively the peg or stick may have a groove cut out all round it near the end, and the fine cane is then tied round the peg at this point, and then twisted and finished off as before. (Figure 105.)

Point the other end of the peg.

The stick may be wrapped or left plain, and it may or may not have a handle.

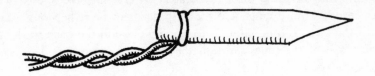

FIGURE 105. TWO FASTENING PEGS

A wooden bead may be attached by a fine cane to form a loop, so placed that the hasp clips over it and is held.

A More Elaborate Hasp

Shape a piece of No. 15 cane, well soaked, into a figure of 8, without crossing the cane over. Make the join in the same way as the small wrapped handle—see page 74. Arrange the join so that it comes into the waist of the 8. You may find it easier to make the loops round something solid. The bodkin handle will give two different size circles. Dry the cane in the required position held with a clothes peg and then glue the join and wrap with fuse wire. (Figure 106.)

Wrap the centre section with a very fine chair seating cane starting and finishing in the same way as for a partly wrapped handle—see page 66. (Figure 107.)

Attach the hasp to the basket in the same way as the small wrapped handle on page 77.

A More Elaborate Fastening Peg

This goes well with the previous hasp. Make an elongated loop in No. 15 cane, well soaked, bringing both ends together and lying in the same direction. (Figure 108.) Glue the ends together and wire them, and cut them off so that the peg measures about $1\frac{1}{2}$ in–2 in. Wrap the glued ends for about $\frac{3}{4}$ in. Attach this in with the loop. To fasten the basket, thread the peg through the hasp and then turn sideways so that it is held tightly between the loop and the hasp. (Figure 109.) Experiment to see that the loop is tight enough, but not so tight that it will be torn away in use.

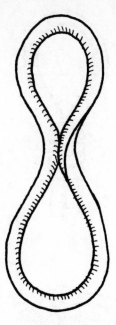

FIGURE 106. A MORE ELABORATE HASP

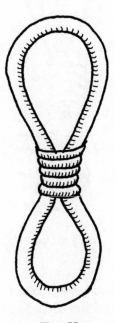

FIGURE 107. THE HASP COMPLETED

FIGURE 108. A MORE ELABORATE PEG

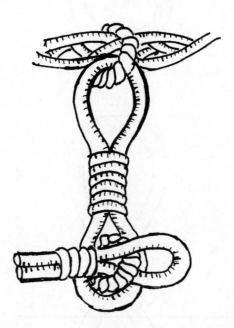

FIGURE 109. THE PEG AND HASP IN PLACE

HINGES

Hinges are really very simple and mostly consist of a piece of flat or round, cane or willow, binding the borders of the lid and the siding together, and then each end of this cane is woven away.

There are however some points to watch that will help you.

1. Don't make this binding too tight or too loose.

2. Both the ends must be woven away on the same piece of the work, i.e. both on the lid or both on the siding.

3. If there are 2 or more hinges, see that each one has the same number of turns to the binding.

4. If there are 2 or more hinges the same piece of cane may be carried on to the next hinge (woven in, of course).

5. If one border catches against the other, bind one of the borders, just at this point, with fine chair seating cane before you put the hinge on.

6. To hinge a square lid through the thick side sticks, provision must be made in the construction of the lid—see page 88.

7. The hinge on a round lid must be very short or the lid will be clamped down. For greater stability add a plaited or twisted stay, on each side of the hinge. See below.

Plaited or Twisted Stay Hinge

Not really a hinge at all but put on to help the bound hinge, or sometimes used merely to join the lid to the basket to avoid loss.

Put on exactly as a loop, starting on the outside of the lid and finishing below the border of the siding, so that it is quite tight when the lid is closed.

A similar twist or plait of fine cane may be put on the inside of the basket to prevent the lid from opening too far.

COVERS OR LIDS

There are 3 types of lids:

(1) Those that rest on a ledge just inside the basket.

(2) Those that fit exactly on to the border of the siding and are hinged and fastened to keep them in place.

(3) Those that fit over the edge of the siding and have an upsett of their own, and may be hinged or not.

THE LEDGE AND INSIDE FITTING LID

Suitable for round or oval baskets.

The ledge can be made in 2 ways,

1. Put on a trac border finishing to the inside. Pair 2 or 3 rounds using the ends of the border stakes as stakes, making sure that they point to the centre of the basket as much as possible. Finish off with trac border No. 1 or 2. (Figure 110.)

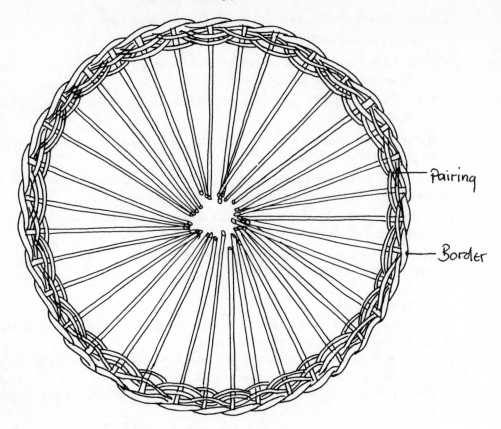

Pairing

Border

FIGURE 110. BORDER STAKES READY TO MAKE A LEDGE FOR A LID

2. About $\frac{1}{2}$ in–1 in before the border put on a round of 4 or 5-rod waling inside out. That is, in front of one and behind 3 (or 4) instead of the normal way. Or you could do the round of waling on the inside if the basket were large enough. See that the remainder of the siding flows out slightly from this round so that the lid can be placed inside easily. This second method is particularly suitable for willow and hedgerow basketry.

THE LID

The lid, round or oval, is made in a very similar way to the base with these differences.

1. It can, but need not, be domed, or the dome can be accentuated to form a deep lid.

2. Fancy weaving can be put on in the lid, and it is usual to put on a few rounds of waling at the edge.

3. Extra sticks can be added after the cross to get a closer weave, especially at the edge.

4. Bye-sticks can be added for a sturdier lid.

Finish the lid with a trac or 3-rod border, making sure that the ends are finished to the inside of the lid. If a 3-rod border is put on with the outside or right side of the lid facing you, and this means that the ends will finish on top, then complete the border with a follow-on trac, tucking the ends to the other side of the lid.

The border stakes may be added after the weaving is completed and inserted to the left of each stake, so that the border stakes turn down over the ends of the sticks. If the sticks are rather far apart, one border stake may be added on each side of each stick end. Cane workers making a small lid, may cut the cover sticks long enough in the first place to complete the border. (This would not be possible with willow or hedgerow because of the difference in thickness between tip and butt.)

Never have the border stakes of a lid thicker than No. 5 cane, or the equivalent size in willow or hedgerow, and preferably No. 3, or even less, otherwise the border will be clumsy.

Don't forget to allow room for your border when you are measuring the lid—it will add another $\frac{3}{4}$ in–1 in on the diameter.

Finish your lid by adding some form of handle.

The Hinged Lid

The round and oval lids are made exactly as before (finishing only with a rod border making quite sure that the lid fits exactly. Add the hinges and the fastenings afterwards.

The square lid is a little more difficult, as:

1. Your square (cornered) basket probably hasn't finished up with very square corners at the top.

2. Provision has to be made for the hinges in construction of the lid.

3. Only the ends are bordered.

Let's cope with 1, first. Cut a cardboard pattern of the lid. You can do this by turning the basket upside down and drawing round it onto the cardboard. I'm sure that you will have something like Figure 111. (If it comes out perfectly square at the corners, then start and finish just as you did the base.) Now cut $\frac{3}{8}$ in from each end which will be taken up by the border. Mark on the template exactly where the hinges are to come.

Set the cover sticks up in the screwlock—see Figure 112, measure against the template and allow approximately $\frac{1}{8}$ in on the outside of the thick edge sticks, which will be taken up with the weaving canes or rods. When using cane you may double all the sticks or alternatively just the thick outside ones, for a sturdier lid. (If you are working in willow or hedgerow, you would merely take thicker sticks to make it sturdier.) If you do decide

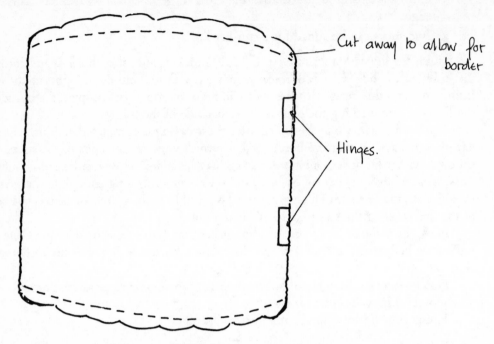

FIGURE 111. TEMPLATE FOR A SQUARE LID

on double stakes on the outside refer to page 91, Method 3 before setting up the sticks in the block.

Put in the first row which will be pairing in exactly the same way as for the base. Now place the template at the back of the work and lift up the pairing row at the corners to match the template and pad them underneath with some odd pieces of cane or willow. (Figure 112.) Fill in the dip with randing. (Figure 113.) Once the randing goes straight across, continue as you did for the base.

The end is made by padding the middle of the weaving, again to match the template, and finish with a row of pairing right across.

Work now until the first hinge mark is approaching.

2. *Provision for the Hinges*
There are three ways of making provision for the hinges, or hinge marks.

Method 1. Used when there is only one outside stick and the inner sticks are not too widely spaced. When the weaving is up to the beginning of the first space, take the weaver round the first inner stick instead of the outside stick. Continue to weave like this until the length of the space is reached and then go back to weaving round the outside stick until the next hinge mark is reached. (Figure 114.)

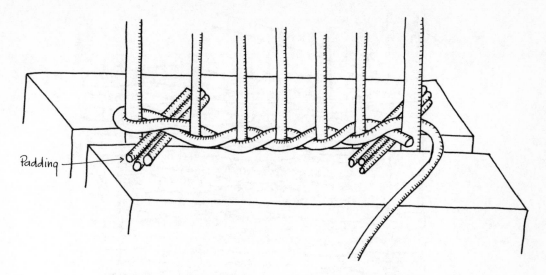

Padding

FIGURE 112. PADDING THE LID TO MATCH THE TEMPLATE

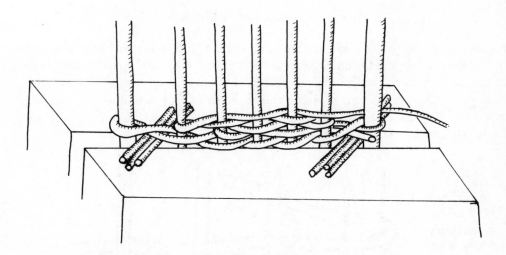

FIGURE 113. FILLING IN THE 'DIP' WITH RANDING

Method 2. Exactly the same as for the previous one, but if this would leave too big a gap in the lid, insert a small piece of rod or cane (the same size as the inner sticks) into the randing, between the outer stick and the first inner stick, about 2 in before the hinge space is started. Don't allow this extra stick to get too close to the outer stick (it will try to!),

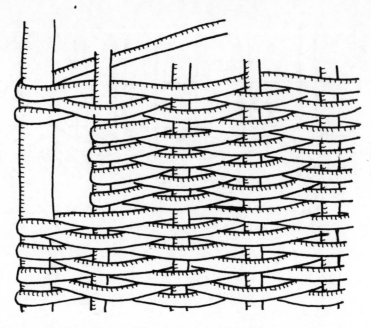

FIGURE 114. HINGE SPACE—METHOD 1

use a bodkin or a wedge or even another piece of cane to keep it sufficiently far away to allow for the randing and the hinge. (Figure 115.) Continue to rand up to the hinge mark, keeping the extra stick firmly in place. When the hinge mark is reached, remove the bodkin or wedges and pass the weaving round the extra stick intead of the outer stick. (Figure 116.) When the space is long enough, go back to weaving round the outer stick, but leave the extra stick in for another 2 in.

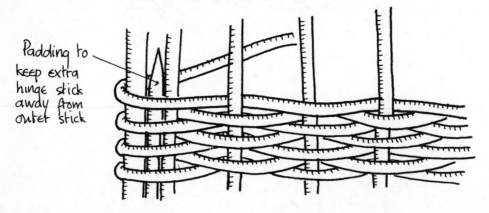

Padding to keep extra hinge stick away from outer stick

FIGURE 115. HINGE SPACE—METHOD 2

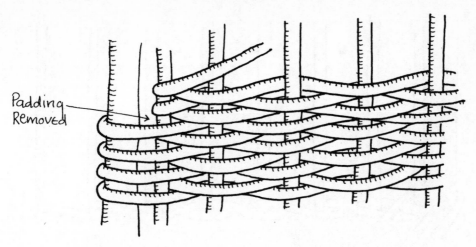

FIGURE 116. HINGE SPACE—CONTINUATION OF METHOD 2

Method 3. Used when the outer sticks are doubled. Before the sticks are set up in the block, the hinge spaces must be *cut* on the inner of the 2 thick sticks, sufficiently deep to allow for the randing of the cover and the actual hinge. Use the template for the guidance

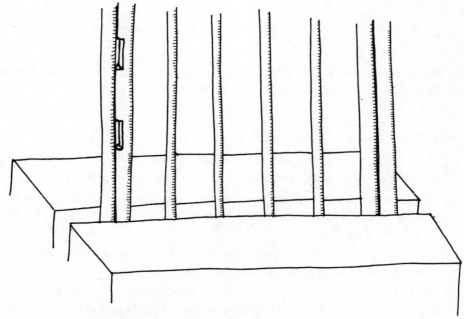

FIGURE 117. HINGE SPACE—METHOD 3

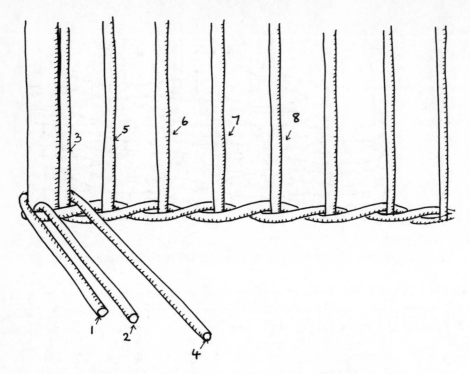

FIGURE 118. STARTING THE BORDER OF A SQUARE LID (1)

of the spaces. Set the sticks up in the block as in Figure 117, and when you reach the first hinge space, pass the weaver round the cut of the inner thick stick.

3. *The Border of the Square lid: a 3-rod border*

   1. Remove the work from the block and pick off. Replace it in the block for support and border the finishing end first.

   2. With the WRONG side of the work towards you, leave the corner sticks standing but cut off all the inner ones close to the work, and slype and insert a border stake to the left of each one.

   3. Slype and insert 2 stakes by the left hand corner stick, one to the right side and one to the front which is bent down to the front.

   4. Wrap an 8 in piece of cane round or rod round this same outer stick, so that the right end is about 5 in and the left end is about 3 in. (Figure 118.) I have numbered these stakes 1 to 8 in the explanation, for clarity.

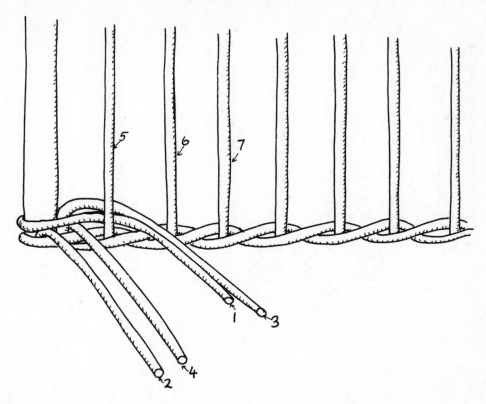

FIGURE 119. STARTING THE BORDER OF A SQUARE LID (2)

5. Nip or prick down all the stakes except the 8 in piece which you laid round the corner stick.

You are now ready to start the border. Be careful to keep to the shape of the template and don't allow the corners to rise up.

1. Starting at the left hand side, pass 1 behind 5 and back to the front again to lie in front of 6.
2. Bend down 3 to lie beside and behind 1. (Figure 119.)
3. Pass 2 in front of 5 and behind 6 and back to the front to lie in front of 7.
4. Bend down 5 to lie beside and behind 2. (Figure 120.)
5. Pass 4 in front of 6 and behind 7 and back to the front to lie in front of 8.
6. Bend down 6 to lie beside and behind 4. (Figure 121.)

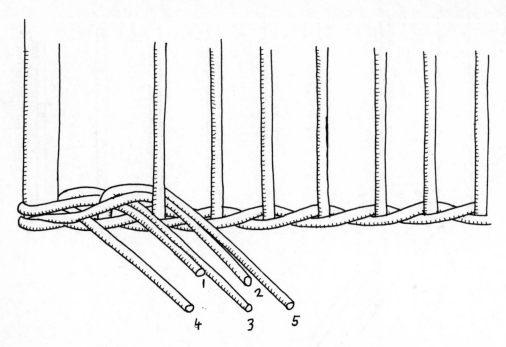

FIGURE 120. STARTING THE BORDER OF A SQUARE LID (3)

You should now have 3 pairs lying to the front and can continue with a normal 3-rod border (remember—5th stake from the right, in front of one and behind one and the upright down behind it) until you have only one stake still upright, and the right hand pair lies against the right corner stick.

To Finish

1. Pass the 5th stake from the right, in front of the last remaining upright stake and behind and *right round* the corner stick.

2. Thread it through to the right side of the work, just under the border. (Figure 122.)

3. Bend down the last stake and wrap that also round the corner stick, on the outside of the previous stake, and thread this also through to the right side of the work, in the same place. (Figure 123.)

4. Hammer in a small nail through these last 2 stakes and into the corner stick, making sure that the border is pressed down well enough to match the template. (Figure 124.)

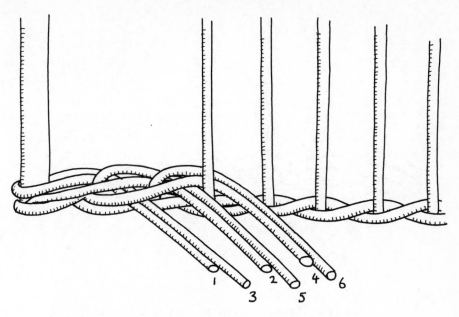

FIGURE 121. STARTING THE BORDER OF A SQUARE LID (4)

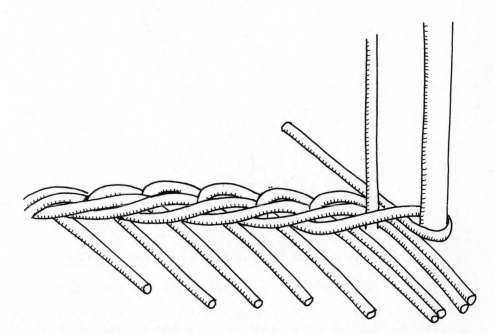

FIGURE 122. FINISHING THE BORDER OF A SQUARE LID (1)

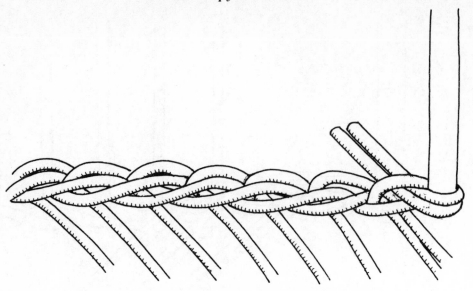

FIGURE 123. FINISHING THE BORDER OF A SQUARE LID (2)

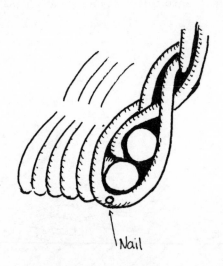

Nail

FIGURE 124. FINISHING THE BORDER OF A SQUARE LID (3)

5. Hammer a small nail in the similar place on the other corner stake.

6. Weave away one or both of the stakes lying on the right side of the lid, to the wrong side. If only one is woven away as is usual in willow choose the left hand one and pick off the other very close on the right side.

7. Pick off all the stakes that lie on the wrong side of the lid, i.e. the side that was facing you while you were bordering.

8. Saw the corner stakes off, or cut cleanly with sharp shears, as close to the border as possible.

9. Repeat the process at the other end.

If the cover is rather large, or it is on an article that is going to take a great deal of handling, you may bind the border in one or two places with a skein of willow or some chair seating cane.

Insert the cane into the randing, about 1 in down and wrap over the border and through the randing 9 or 10 times, making a fan shape. (Figure 125.)

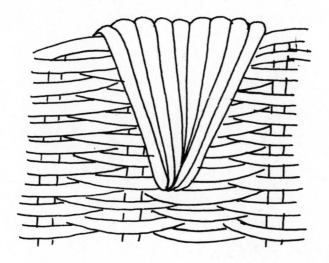

FIGURE 125. BINDING THE BORDER OF A SQUARE LID

Alternatively, whip the border evenly for the whole width, passing over the border once for every stake. Tough leather thonging is often used for this process.

The Cover with a Flange

When using a cover with a flange it is best to finish the siding of the basket with a trac border falling slightly inwards (number 4 trac is very suitable) as this avoids the need to have the lid very large in order to avoid 'catching' the borders.

Make your cover as before, but instead of putting on a border, stake up and upsett just as you would for the base of the basket.

The depth of the flange will depend on the number of rounds of waling you put on. Keep this flange very straight and finish with a normal 3 rod border.

Be careful not to make the lid too big before the upsett. Remember that the upsett will add ¾ in–1 in on to the diameter of the lid.

This lid may be hinged and fastened. If this is required, make the last round of the waling on the basket, a 4 or 5 rod wale, and put the hinge binding through this waling on the outside of the basket only, and the border of the lid.

6. Bases, Staking Up & the Upsett

MOST BASKETS are either round, oval or square. Square refers to the right angle of the corner, and in actual fact a 'square' basket is nearly always rectangular. The shape of a basket is determined by the shape of the base. A round base may finish up oval, as in the case of a bucket bag, but nevertheless, it is still a round basket.

Round baskets are much the easiest to make and many of these should be tried before 'graduating' to oval and then on to square.

Always remember that the sticks of the base are the thickest of the basket and the weavers of the base are the finest.

Although bases can be made to any reasonable size (i.e. in relation to and suitable for basketry) there is nearly always a tendency to make it too large for the basket required.

The number, thickness and length of the base sticks will depend on the size of the basket—see Chapter 7—on design. Bases should always be concave if possible, in order to give the basket strength (on the principle of the arch) but this is not possible in the case of square bases nor in flower arranging baskets which will need a flat bottom to keep a water container steady. Concave bases are not necessary in baskets that literally take no weight, i.e. an Easter egg container.

The best way to learn to make your own base is to do one, and instructions are given in the next few pages for a small base of each shape and how to stake up and upsett them.

ROUND BASES

It is not necessary to have an even number of base sticks and when an odd number is used, always pierce one less than the number to be threaded through.

The minimum number of sticks that can be used on a round base is 5. When only 4 are used the base never seems to come 'round' but remains 'squarish'.

Instructions are given for a round cane base and a round willow base, each suitable for a child's basket or a small flower arranging basket.

A Small Round Cane Base

1. Cut 6 bottom sticks of prepared No. 8 cane, 6 in long.
2. Pierce 3 in the centre with the bodkin or knife.
3. Sharpen the other 3 at one end and thread these through the 3 pierced canes so that it forms a single cross. (Figure 126.)

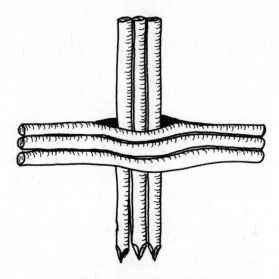

FIGURE 126. THE CROSS OF A ROUND BASE

4. Begin the weaving, which is pairing, with one long piece of No. 3 cane, doubled roughly in the middle. (To avoid cracking this weaving cane hold it in the first two fingers and the thumb of each hand, quite close together, and twist each hand in the opposite direction until the fibres part. The cane will now bend right over without breaking.)
5. Loop this bend over one arm of the cross, with both ends to the front. (Figure 127.)
6. Pair for 2 rounds, turning the base round a quarter turn with each stroke. (Figure 128.) (Remember always to use the weaver on the left, and it must pass *over* the other one on its journey to the back. The base will be much tighter and firmer if the weaver is pulled down while it is at the *back* of the work before slipping it to the front: Don't pull down at the front or the sticks will become distorted, whereas they never do when pulled down at the back. It will help also if the right hand weaver, that is, the one that is lying idle for the moment, is held down by the left thumb.)

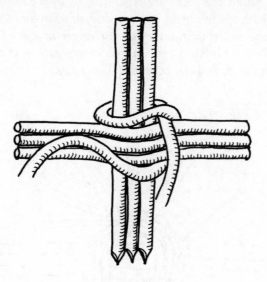

FIGURE 127. STARTING THE BASE PAIRING, OR TYING IN THE SLATH

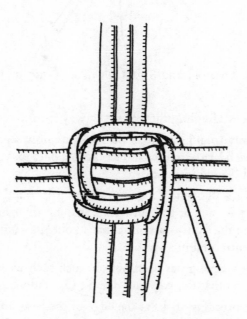

FIGURE 128. PAIRING FOR TWO ROUNDS

7. On the next round the sticks are separated, or opened out, to look like spokes of a wheel. With the left hand weaver, do half a stroke so that it lies at the back of the base, and with the thumb and forefinger of the left hand, pull the next stick away from the other 2 and slip the weaver that is at the back, to the front in between this stick and the other 2. (Figure 129.)

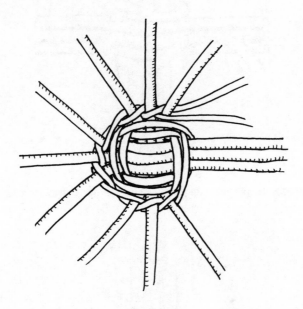

FIGURE 129. OPENING THE STICKS OUT, OR TYING IN THE SLATH

8. Repeat this process dividing the 3rd stick away from the centre one.

9. Repeat all the way round so that all the sticks are now separated. Try to keep the centre stick of each 'arm' straight and let the side ones move outwards. This whole process is called 'Tying in the Slath'.

10. Once the sticks are all opened out, continue to pair round until the base measures approximately 5 in, and at the same time shaping the base so that it has a slight curve away from the front—not more than about $\frac{1}{2}$ in – $\frac{3}{4}$ in difference between the edge and the centre. (Figure 130.)

11. When sufficient weaving has been put on, tuck each weaver under the previous row of pairing, so that the weaving doesn't slip undone.

12. Trim off any protruding sticks at the edge of the base, and the ends of the joins, as close as possible, and the base is ready for the upsett.

FIGURE 130.

Round Base in Willow or Hedgerow

Basically the same as for cane but there are one or two 'differences' that must be made clear.

Refer to page 12, to learn how to grade and select the rods for use.

Remember that fewer stakes, and therefore fewer bottom sticks are required for a willow or hedgerow basket than for a similar sized one in cane. Therefore start your very first willow base with only 5 bottom sticks. (The cane one had 6.)

1. Cut 5 sticks about 6 in long from the butt ends of 5 of the stoutest rods in your bundle. (Of course, for such a small basket they would not need to be very stout, no more than say No. 10 cane.)

2. Pierce 2 in the centre and pass the other 3 through them to form one cross, as in the cane base.

3. Hold the cross in the left hand so that the 3 sticks are upright and the 2 sticks are horizontal.

4. Take 2 thin rods of roughly equal length, from the pile that you have selected for base weaving.

5. Insert both tips, with any wispy cracked ends cut off, into the split that was formed by the piercing, and to the left of the 3 upright sticks, and bend these rods down to the front. (Figure 131.)

6. Take one of them round the back of the 3 sticks and down to the front on the right side of this 'arm'. It is now ready for pairing. (Figure 132.)

7. Continue now as for the cane base, except that when there are 3 sticks to open out in willow, only separate the left one on the first opening round and the right one on the second, or next round.

8. Pair out to the required size, remembering to make the base slightly concave, and pick off the base and cut off any surplus stick ends.

For Willow & Cane Workers

Try to get the pairing weavers as close to the centre as possible, especially when opening out. As this is probably the most difficult part of a round basket, do not be discouraged at first if your base looks a little untidy or loose. After you have had a little practice it will improve. REMEMBER TO PULL THE WEAVER WELL DOWN AT THE BACK BEFORE SLIPPING IT TO THE FRONT.

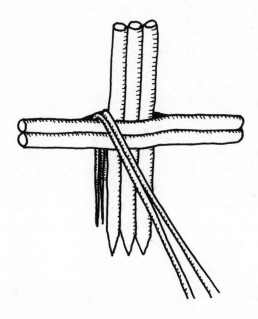

FIGURE 131. STARTING THE ROUND BASE IN WILLOW (1)

Staking Up the Round Cane Base

The number of side stakes required is twice the number of base stick ends, less one.

Having cut the stakes the required length, according to the pattern or design, soak a few inches at one end and slype them at the dampened end. Insert them one on either side of each bottom stick end except one, which only has one stake beside it. (Figure 133.) This is to form an odd number of stakes which makes randing and slewing so much easier later.

Place the base *concave side up* on the table to stake up, so that it is not squashed or distorted, although this is the under side of the basket. It must be turned over before the next stage.

See that the stakes go right into the centre of the base, using the bodkin to help by forming a channel first; otherwise the basket will be weak.

NIP each stake at the edge of the base with the round nosed pliers so that they bend up easily without cracking.

At this stage we either tie the stakes together at the top or put on a hoop of the required size and shape, to keep the stakes in order during the upsetting. The tying speaks

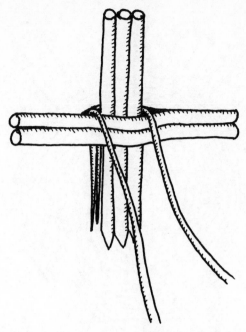

FIGURE 132. STARTING THE ROUND BASE IN WILLOW (2)

for itself and personally I prefer this method as it is so much quicker and easier than the hoop, but once again you must experiment and decide for yourself. See page 7.

THE UPSETT

This is the term given to the place in the basket where it stops going out and starts going up, and until the stakes are firmly held in their new upright position.

The upsett is woven with waling and the first round can be put on with any number of weavers from 3 to 6. The more weavers that are used, the larger the ridge that the basket stands on will be.

Do not lay the weavers in but either insert them into the base weaving or loop them round the stakes.

If the upsett is started with a 3-rod wale, continue on after the first round, but remember to do the *step-up*—see page 16. If, however it is started with a 4-rod wale, one weaver should be dropped at the end of the first round. Then continue with a 3-rod wale. Drop the one that comes out of the space where the first weaver was put in. Don't forget that if a loop was used there will be very little of it showing. (Figure 134.) Do not cut it off too short as it is a good idea to weave it away later. Mark the stake to the left of this space and do a step-up at this point now and every subsequent round.

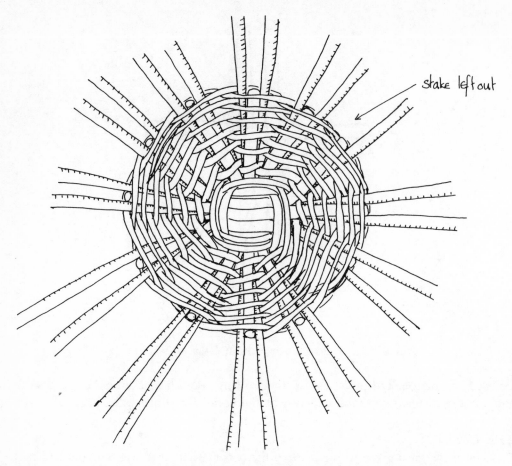

stake left out

FIGURE 133. STAKING UP WITH AN ODD NUMBER OF STAKES

With a 5 or 6-rod wale it is better to do one round, finished off completely and then start the 3-rod wale quite separately.

Work the first round of upsetting as closely as possible—the tendency is always for it to splay out more than is required. Try not to have any gaps between the pairing of the base and the first round of the waling.

When the first round of the waling has been done, the basket should be secured in some way to keep it firm and steady; so that it is possible to shape the basket without it constantly tipping up. Many people use a board, lap-board or a plank and, if this is pre-ferred, the basket should be tied to the board or pegged with a bodkin or bradawl through the centre of the base, so that the basket can turn round on the board. Personally I prefer to have my baskets weighted down. I consider that this gives me greater freedom of movement and is easier to manage. I use ordinary boulders from the garden or seaside and so can produce just the right sized 'weight' for the basket of the moment. (The stones can look very gay when brightly painted with poster paints and then varnished.) Old fashioned flat irons, scale-weights or even tins filled with sand can be used.

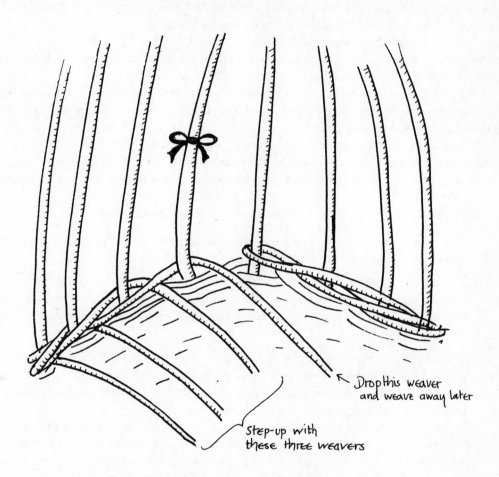

Drop this weaver and weave away later

Step-up with these three weavers

FIGURE 134. WHERE TO PLACE THE STEP-UP

Whether you choose lap-board or plank, string or peg, stones or tins of sand, is a matter of personal preference. It is a good idea to try all methods and then decide which is the most comfortable way of working for you.

Continue now with a 3-rod wale for not less than 2 rounds. Beginners would be better off with 4 or 5. When the stakes are firmly held in the required position the tie or hoop can be removed. The basket is now ready for the siding.

Staking Up and Upsett for Willow & Hedgerow

Select the required number of stakes to be used. These are slyped (see page 5) for 1 in–1½ in at the butt end of the rods.

Now insert the slyped stakes into the base, one on each side of every bottom stick end, less one, as for the cane base, making sure that each stake goes as far as possible into the centre of the base. Use the bodkin to help, and have the base concave side up to avoid squashing or distorting the shape of the base. Make quite sure that all the slype is inside the weaving of the base. Do not trim the stakes at the tip end at all but use the whole rod and only trim after the border has been completed.

The stakes must now be PRICKED-UP before they can be turned up, see page 5, unlike the cane stakes which are merely nipped. Be sure to turn the base over before you prick-up or it will be the wrong way round.

When all the stakes have been pricked-up, gather them all up and tie or hoop them as for a cane basket. Make sure that the stakes are already 'sitting' straight and level. If any of the 'elbows' of the stakes appear to be too far out from the base, they can be rapped in with the iron.

The upsett is very much the same as for the cane base except that:

1. The willow cannot be looped round the stakes, therefore all the weavers must be inserted into the base weaving, and

2. There is no step-up in willow work. When upsetting with a 4-rod wale and continuing with only 3, drop whichever is the most convenient when the first round is complete, e.g. if one is getting very thick or is broken, then that will be the one to drop.

The upsett can be started with tips or butts. It is easier to start with the tips, but with a heavy basket the butts would be more in keeping. Or about 12 in could be trimmed from the tip ends so that they are not too fine. Slype the butts before inserting. Always use rods of similar size and length and join in butts to butts and tips to tips.

Never join in on the first round of the upsett as this would weaken the basket badly. If the rods are not long enough to go right round the base and overlap at least a few inches (and yet still be finer at the butt ends than the side stakes), start the upsett in 2 places, on opposite sides of the basket. Let each set of weavers go past, and on top of the other, and join in both sets to continue until the upsett is complete. This shouldn't be necessary for a round base, but is always used with a square and an oval base unless they are very small.

Always finish the upsett with the tips of the rods to give a smooth 'run down' ending.

OVAL BASE

Oval-based work is more advanced than round and it should not be attempted too soon. Make plenty of round bases first to become thoroughly proficient.

All oval bases have a great tendency to twist (although care should be taken to keep this to a minimum) and a reverse pair is put on, as well as pairing to counteract this twist.

The bottom sticks of an oval base are 2 different lengths, which are referred to as the long sticks and the short sticks. Please turn to page 124 to work out how many and what length they should be for a particular size.

A Small Oval Cane Base

Cut 4 sticks 10 in long and 7 sticks 6 in long, of No. 10 cane. Pierce the short sticks in the centre and thread the long ones through. Arrange them as in Figure 135 with 1 in spaces between the short sticks, and making quite sure that the distance from A–B and C–B is the same.

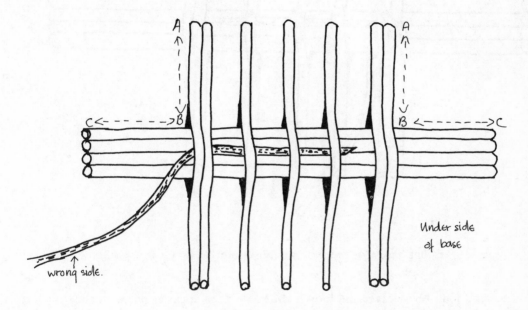

FIGURE 135. STARTING THE WRAPPING OF THE OVAL BASE

It is usual in good quality canework, although not essential, to bind these sticks in place.

Insert a piece of No. 4 chair seating cane, or for coarser work glossy wrapping may be used, wrong side towards you, into the splits of the short sticks, on the underside of the base. (Figure 135.) Make a cross round the 2 end short sticks. See Figures 136 and 137 showing the top and under sides at this point. Continue by wrapping the long sticks with the same number of laps in each space. The wrapping must be firm and taut, but not so tight that the long sticks become bunched up. Finish with a cross similar to the beginning and thread the cane a little way down behind the wrapping on the underside of the base. Use a bodkin to help you. See Figures 137 and 138 showing upper and lower sides.

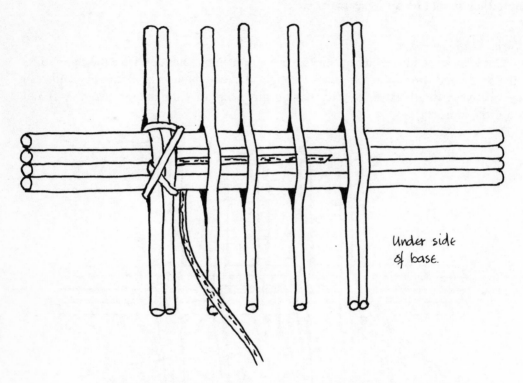

FIGURE 136. CONTINUING THE WRAPPING OF AN OVAL BASE

Select a long fine weaver and loop it round the long sticks at one end, and pair for 2 rounds, keeping the pairing close to the wrapping: see Figures 139 and 140 showing the right and the wrong way of working. On the third round open the 4 long sticks to pairs at each end and on the 6th round open all the pairs including the end short sticks. Bend the outer short stick at each end towards the curve of the base and keep the other very straight. Try to keep all the other short sticks very straight and do not allow them to lean to one side. Continue to pair until slightly less than half the required weaving is put on, at the same time making the base slightly concave as in the round base. Try hard to allow as little twist as possible. (Figure 141.)

Now change to reverse pairing (see page 23) for half the weaving, which should counteract the twist. Remembering that less than half was paired in the first instance, there

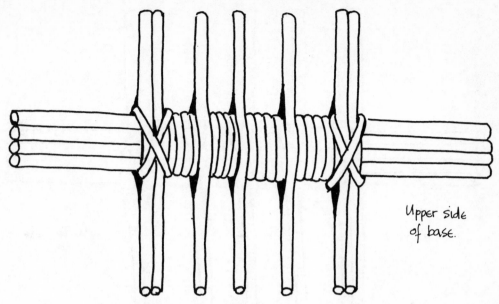

Upper side
of base.

FIGURE 137. THE BASE WRAPPING ON THE UPPER SIDE

will now be enough room to revert to pairing for 3 or 4 rounds at the edge of the base. Secure the ends of the weavers and clip off all the surplus protruding ends of the sticks and the base is ready for the staking up.

The more experienced cane worker may prefer to weave the oval base with chain pairing—i.e. one round of pairing and one round of reverse pairing. This looks extremely attractive when it is done well. An example can be seen in Plate 12.

Start the base as before by looping the cane round the long sticks at one end and pair only along one side. Loop a second weaver round the long sticks at the other end and reverse pair with these weavers along both sides, but do not overtake the first weavers. Now revert to the first weavers and pair one round, then change to the second weavers and reverse pair for one round, and so on. Still remember to open out the sticks at the right time, and make the base concave. There should be no twist this time as it is being counteracted all the time.

An Oval Base in Willow

An oval base in willow is worked in exactly the same way as for cane except that:

1. The long sticks are seldom bound, only a basket of very fine quality would be improved by binding, and then a willow skein would be used.

2. Chain pairing is never put on a willow basket; the oval base is always woven with blocks of pairing and reverse pairing.

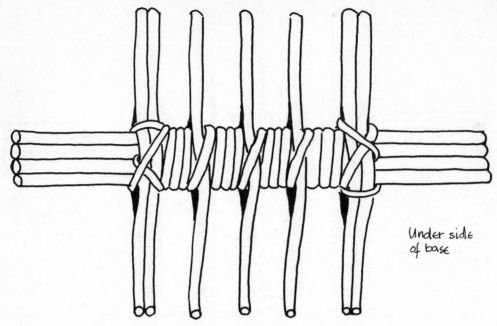

Under side
of base

FIGURE 138. THE BASE WRAPPING ON THE UNDER SIDE

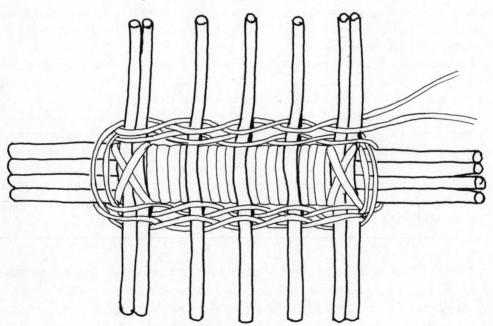

FIGURE 139. THE CORRECT WAY TO PAIR AN OVAL BASE WITH THE
WEAVING CLOSE TO THE WRAPPING

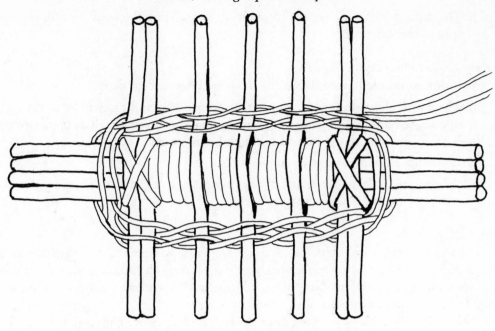

FIGURE 140. THE INCORRECT WAY TO PAIR AN OVAL BASE WITH THE WEAVING LOOSE

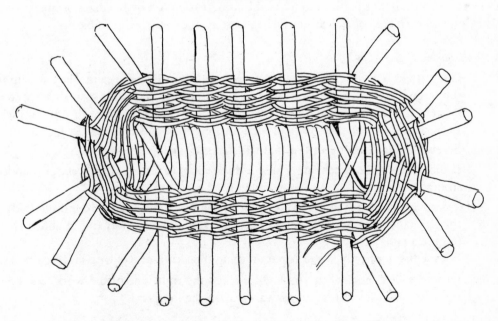

FIGURE 141. OPENING THE STICKS OF AN OVAL BASE

3. The pairing is started, like the round base, by inserting the weaving rods into the split of the short sticks.

Staking Up and Upsetting an Oval Base
This process is exactly the same as for the round base except that:

1. The *straight* short sticks only have a stake on one side, and this will go to the right side of the bottom stick as you are staking up—that is with the base upside down. Remember to finish up with an odd number of stakes.

2. If you use a hoop, it must be an oval one.

3. When using willow it is nearly always necessary to use 2 sets of weavers for the waling of the upsett, refer to page 108.

SQUARE BASES
For square work a screwblock is used see page 3. It is more difficult than round or oval, mainly because it has a great tendency to twist during the upsett so that the border does not finish straight with the base, and unlike the oval base, there is nothing to counter-act it except the skill of the worker.

There are 2 methods of working once the base is completed. The corners can be left sharp and square by inserting a thick rod or piece of cane exactly at the corners on the first round of the upsett. Although this is attractive it is rather advanced. The other method, which is described in this book, is to make the corners roundish by having 2 ordinary sized stakes, one on each side of the corner and as close to the corner as possible.

A Small Square Base in Cane
1. Cut 5 sticks 9 in long of No. 12 cane and 2 of 8 mm handle cane. Set these up in the screwblock with the large sticks on the outside and with spaces of approximately 1 in between each stick. (Figure 142.). In order to make the larger sticks fit in the block with the rest, cut sections from one end. (Figure 143.)

2. Screw the block up tightly so that the sticks are held very firmly.

3. If the base is to be much larger, use 2 thick sticks together, at each end, for added strength.

4. Take a good long weaver of No. 3 or No. 5 cane, and loop it round the stick at the left hand edge, so that there is one long end and one short end of about 12 in. (Figure 144.)

5. For the first row only, a pair is put on using the 2 ends of this weaver. (Figure 145.)

6. Drop the short end when you have reached the right side of the work, and continue to rand backwards and forwards, with the long end.

To avoid 'grins' or spaces on the outer sticks, the weaver may be taken *twice* round the outside sticks. You may find that it is not necessary every time, but perhaps the extra twist is needed 2 out of every 3 rows, or every other one. But whichever one you do, keep it the same all the way up. The closer the randing, the less often you will need the extra twist.

Join in at the back of the work, and never too close to the outer sticks.

Take care not to:

1. let the sticks fall in or spread out,
2. let them all lean over to one side,
3. let the inner sticks fall backwards or forwards.

To help to avoid the first 2 mistakes, a gauge is very useful. You can make one with a piece of cane or stick. Make 2 cuts in a piece of thickish cane, about 10 in long in this

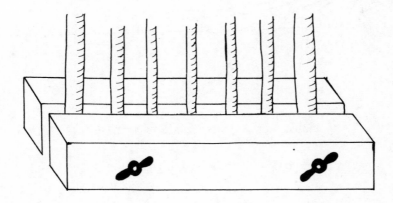

FIGURE 142. SETTING THE STICKS IN THE SCREWBLOCK FOR SQUARE WORK

case, and bend the ends round so that the centre section measures exactly the same as the width of the base. (Figure 146.)

By constant use of this gauge, it will be seen if the base is getting wider or narrower. Another method is to tie or nail a piece of cane right across the top of the sticks and so keep them steady, but I find this is rather restricting, especially for small willow work.

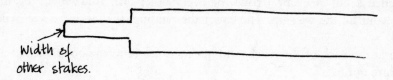

Width of
other stakes.

FIGURE 143. HOW TO CUT THE LARGE OUTER STICKS TO FIT INTO THE
SCREWBLOCK

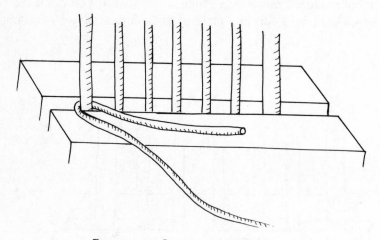

FIGURE 144. STARTING THE SQUARE BASE

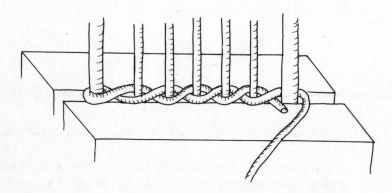

FIGURE 145. THE FIRST ROW OF THE SQUARE BASE

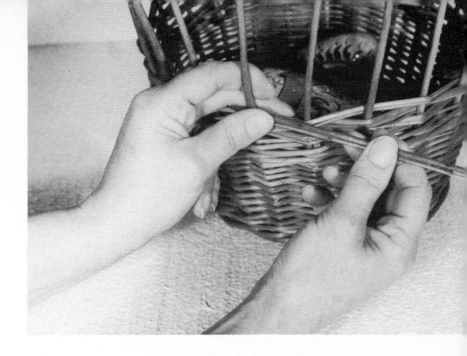

Plate 1   *Showing the position of the left hand for Randing and Slewing. See page 28.*
Note the painted stones inside the basket. See page 107

Plate 2   *Helping the handle rods through the bow. See page 59*

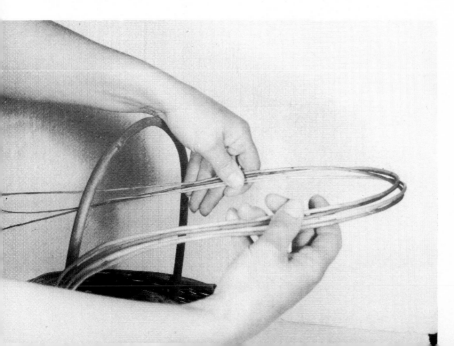

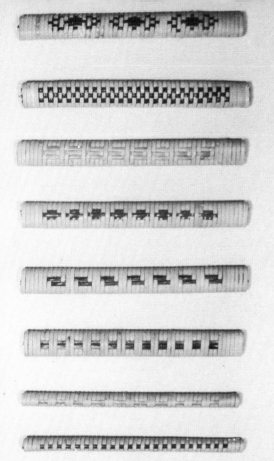

Plate 3   Various Leader Patterns. See page 62

Plate 4   My Scrap book. See page 121

Plate 5   *Wastepaper baskets. Instructions on page 131*

Plate 6   *Easter Egg or Bridesmaids' Baskets. Instructions on page 132*

Plate 7 *Child's Basket in Cane and Seagrass.*
Instructions on page 134

Plate 8 *Three Lampshades in cane. Instructions on pages 135 to 138*

Plate 9   Hanging Flower Basket in cane. Instructions on page 139

Plate 10   Christmas bells in cane. Instructions on page 142

Plate 11   Oval Shopping basket in cane. Instructions on page 140

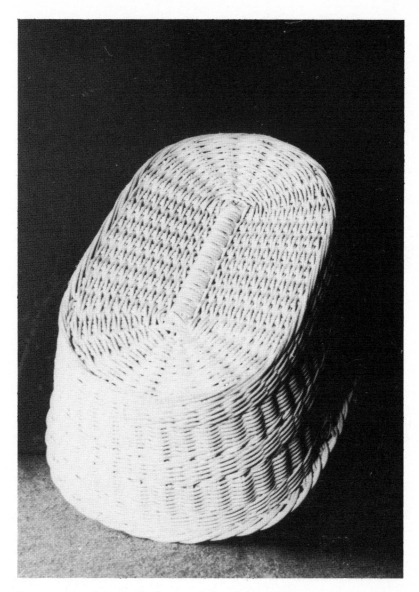

Plate 12   Base of the Oval Shopping basket showing Chain Pairing. See page 111

Plate 13   Cornucopia in cane. Instructions on page 145

*Plate 14   Jack-in-a-box in cane, instructions on page 146:
and Pin-Cushion in Willow, instructions on page 155*

Plate 15   Hat Box in Cane. Instructions on page 148

Plate 16   The hat box open to show child's hat. Instructions on page 151

Plate 17   Tray in willow, instructions on page 151. Covered pots, instructions on page 166

Plate 18   Buff willow Blackberry basket, instructions on page 152. Buff and white willow oval shopping basket, instructions on page 160

Plate 19   Buff willow flower basket. Instructions on page 154

Plate 20   Toy cat basket in buff willow. Instructions on page 156

Plate 21   *White and buff willow round shopping basket.*
Instructions on page 158

Plate 22   *Doll's cradle in buff willow. Instructions on page 161*

Plate 23   The doll's cradle with bed linen

Plate 24   Bird Cage in white willow and Palembang cane.
Instructions on page 163

Plate 25   The bird cage used as a flower basket

Plate 26　An Edwardian Gig in miniature work

Plate 27　An Edwardian Gig from the back

Plate 28   Circus cage in buff willow

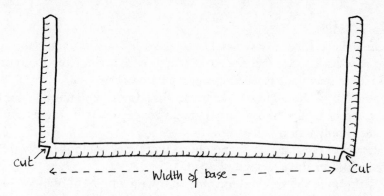

FIGURE 146. A GAUGE FOR MEASURING SQUARE WORK

Continue to the size required and end as you began with one row of pairing. (Figure 147.) After the last row of randing is done, pass the weaver round the end stick (preferably the left one, but it doesn't matter if you can work backwards) and back to the front. Now pass it behind the 2nd stick and put it under the previous row of randing as it comes to the front. Now pass it in front of the 3rd stick and behind the 4th, again passing it under the previous row on its way to the front. Continue like this right across the row, until the weaver lies against the other outer stick. Either cut the weaver off or tuck it down in the weaving.

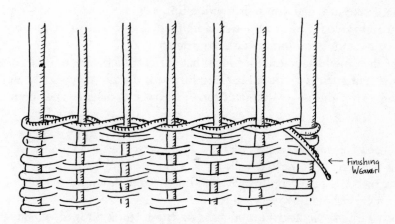

FIGURE 147. FINISHING THE SQUARE BASE WITH ONE ROW OF PAIRING

The base is now removed from the block and picked off; it is now ready for staking.

A Square Base in Willow

Much the same as for the cane base; once again fewer sticks and stakes are required for the same sized basket. See that the sticks that you choose for the base are reasonably straight before you start your base. See paragraph 20 on page 128.

The edge sticks of the willow square base would not be doubled as for cane, but a thicker rod would be used. This is because good strong thick willow is available, whereas the largest cane is only 8 mm or 10 mm.

Cut your sticks as for cane, allowing only 4 inner sticks of moderately thick stuff and 2 rather thick sticks for the edges, all of 10 in.

Set the sticks up in the block as for cane, allowing 1 in–1¼ in between each.

As for cane, start the base with one row of pairing; place the first weaver in the first space on the left, with the tip protruding about 12 in at the back. Bring this end round the back of the end stick to the front, round the back of the 2nd stick and to the front again. Continue pairing to the end of the row, then take the tip of the weaver, round the right-hand stick and weave it away. Now take the other end round the right-hand stick and continue to rand backwards and forwards.

Join in butts to butts and tips to tips, at the back of the work. (An alternative method of joining in on a square base is to join in with the tips each time, inserting them into the weaving.) This may be the inside or the outside of the basket, according to the design. A hamper, or any lined basket would have the joins on the inside, whereas a shopper or a linen basket would have them on the outside.

Only turn the weaving rod once round the outer sticks; the grins in a willow square base are not unattractive.

Work to the desired height and finish as before with a pair in exactly the same way as for cane. Make sure that you finish with a tip.

A square base looks most attractive close randed, but remember that once you have decided to close rand, you must continue to do so.

As for the cane base be careful to see that the end sticks don't fall in, or spread out, and that the centre sticks don't fall back or forwards. Ideally they should all remain perfectly upright, but this is very difficult for the learner to achieve and requires plenty of practice.

Staking Up and Upsetting the Square Base

Much the same for cane and willow.

The corners are staked up first by inserting a stake down by the side of each of the thick rods, which should be well soaked.

DO NOT CUT OFF THE PROTRUDING ENDS OF THESE THICK RODS UNTIL AFTER THE STAKES HAVE BEEN TURNED UP.

Next the sides are pierced with a bodkin at regular intervals, starting as close to the corner as possible, and the slyped rods or canes are pushed well into the hole made by the bodkin. Only do one at a time and if you find the stakes difficult to push in, make the hole a lot larger by moving the bodkin round in the hole and use a little soap to help the stakes to slip in.

In cane, make the insertion so that the end of the stake goes into and is lost in the randing. (Figure 148A.)

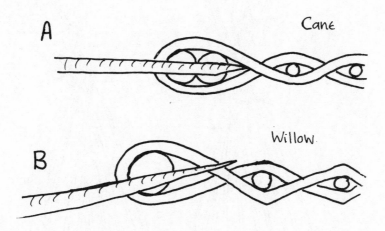

FIGURE 148. THE DIFFERENCE IN STAKING UP IN CANE AND WILLOW

In willow, the insertion goes further in and slightly upwards so that the stake is lying on top of the randing or even on to the next bottom stick. (Figure 148B.)

In both cases great care must be taken to see that none of the slype is still showing on the outside of the base, because this will only crack on the pricking-up.

Make the insertions between the weaving—never piercing the weaving rods or cane.

Finally trim the sticks at the 2 ends of the base and insert one stake beside each. See that these stakes are well into the weaving.

Prick-up or nip the stakes, according to whether they are willow or cane and tie them to secure them in a hoop. The hoop should be oval and not square or oblong, as the stakes tend to collect in the corners. If the tying method is used, it may be easier to tie the stakes into 2 bundles if the base is at all large. (Figure 149.) Do not tie the stakes so tightly that the base is bent upwards. If the stakes are very short, the hoop will be the only possible method.

Cut off the 4 corner sticks now with a good clean cut, made with either a saw or good sharp shears.

The upsett for a square base is exactly the same as for an oval. Choose long weavers in cane to ensure that they will go right round the base with a little to spare. Willow basket makers will almost certainly require 2 sets of weavers, as for a large oval base, which are inserted at each end.

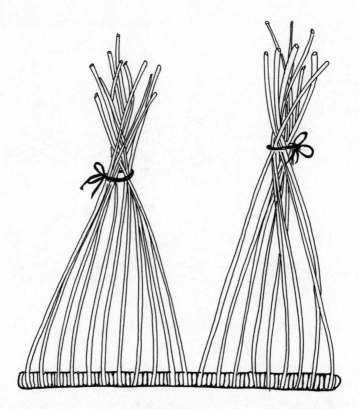

FIGURE 149. TYING THE STAKES OF A SQUARE BASKET IN TWO BUNDLES

7. Planning your basket & starting your own designing

IT'S ALL very well to follow a pattern of a basket exactly, and to a set size, but it may well be that the picnic basket in the book is too big for the Mini (or too small for the Bentley) and anyway you didn't quite want it that shape etc., etc.

In the next few pages I would like to show you how to work out the details of your own basket. How to work out how many stakes you need and how long they should be and so on.

One of the ways that you can really help yourself in your designing is to keep a scrapbook of all the pictures of baskets that you can find in papers and magazines. Not just baskets, but other things that you think one day you may be able to make up in basketry, like the bells for instance on page 142. These pictures will also help you decide on a certain border or handle, and you will be able to see the effects of each from your book. My own scrapbook cover is made from 2 rectangles of willow basketry joined together by 3 'loose-leaf' rings. I can add as many pages of coloured sugar paper inside as I like, when I find new pictures.

I do all my planning and designing at night, during that time when you've woken up and everyone else is asleep (even the children) and all is perfectly quiet. Decide on the object and then the exact shape. Work out the number of stakes and base sticks, in fact run over the whole of the processes from base to border in your mind. You'll be surprised how much time will be saved, and when you get down to work the next day you'll know exactly what to do.

If you are already an experienced basket maker, try very hard to think of examples of basketry (not necessarily 'baskets') that will fit into 20th century living. Try to think of new and exciting ways of using basketry that are interesting and *modern*.

HOW TO WORK OUT THE NUMBERS AND LENGTHS
The first thing you'll ask yourself, of course, is how many base sticks are needed and

how long they should be. But you can't start there. You must start at the border, and you must make up your mind on four things.

1. The shape. Is it to be round, oval or square?
2. The circumference of the basket at the border. This you can easily do by measuring round a bucket or bowl or a basket of similar size. Or you can draw the size on a piece of paper and measure round that. Or you can work out the circumference of a round basket by multiplying the diameter by $3\frac{1}{7}$th, and a square one by adding the measurement of all 4 sides.
3. The thickness of the cane or willow stakes, which must be suitable for the size of the basket and the amount of strength that the basket will have to bear. For instance a work basket or a flower basket would be much daintier and therefore require finer stuff than a shopping basket of the same size.
4. The distance between the stakes, which will depend largely on the size of the stuff and a little on the character of the article. For instance an article that was intended for decoration only, like the Christmas bells on page 142, could have the stakes very wide apart. Perhaps the table below will help and guide you. Please bear in mind that it is very approximate. Remember also, that willow requires fewer stakes, therefore they will be slightly wider apart than for the same size in cane.

Stakes Of:

No. 3 cane—$\frac{1}{4}$ in–$\frac{1}{2}$ in apart.
No. 5 cane—$\frac{1}{2}$ in–$\frac{3}{4}$ in apart.
No. 8 cane—$\frac{3}{4}$ in–1 in apart.
No. 10 cane—1 in–$1\frac{1}{4}$ in apart.
No. 12 cane—$1\frac{1}{4}$ in–$1\frac{1}{2}$ in apart.
No. 15 cane—$1\frac{1}{2}$ in–2 in apart.

These four factors will tell you how many side stakes you will need. Divide the distance between the stakes into the circumference, this will give you the number of stakes and in turn, the number of base sticks, remembering that for a round basket there are 4 stakes (one on each side at each end) to each base stick; and for an oval basket there are 4 stakes to each long stick and the 2 end short ones, and only 2 each for the remaining short ones, but I will be showing you later how to sort out how many short and long sticks to use. A square basket is the easiest to cope with from this point of view, as the stakes are more or less evenly spaced all round except that they are as close as possible at the corners.

The next thing to decide on is again the shape. Not whether it is to be round, or oval, or square this time but whether it is to be short and dumpy or long and thin, and whether the sides will be bowed or straight or flowed, and how high it is to be. Then you must decide on the sort of border you want. These things will tell you the length of the stakes and the base sticks. The length of the stakes will be the sum of three things:

1. The amount needed for the selected border (refer to the chart on page 56).
2. The height of the siding, and
3. The distance from the centre to the edge of the base (except in square work when only 1 in is needed to go into the sides and about 2 in into the ends). Allow an extra inch on these 3 measurements for a bowed siding and 1 in for ease of working.

Lastly before you start you must decide on any accessories and decorations that you think may improve the basket, i.e. lids, handles, fancy weaves etc. If you merely add them as you go along your design may well be out of proportion.

Now let us explore 1 or 2 examples to make sure that we can work these things out.

EXAMPLE NO. 1

Suppose you wanted to make a basket for carrying tea into the garden, and have decided on a round cane basket with a diameter of 16 in, 4 in sides that are quite straight and upright and a wrapped handle of 2 bows, and finally a 4 rod border with a follow on trac No. 2.

As this is quite a large basket, fairly sturdy cane will be required, say No. 12 for the stakes. This means that the base sticks will need to be of No. 14 or 15 cane.

A diameter of 16 in will give a circumference of approximately 50 in. With No. 12 cane, this will mean that the stakes will be about 1¼ in apart and that will give you 40 side stakes, less 1 for the odd number. This in turn will tell you that, because there are 4 side stakes to each base stick, you will start off with 10 base sticks. You will therefore have a cross of 5 by 5.

Your base will also be 16 in as there is to be no flow, so cut the sticks about 17 in to allow for ease of working. (If the basket is to have some flow, then work it all out in the same way but weave the base smaller.)

The length of the stakes will be—7½ in to go right into the centre of the base (leaving 1 in for the cross), 4 in for the siding, 9 in for the 4-rod border, 5 in for the follow on trac and 1 in extra for ease of working, making 26½ in altogether.

So your pattern would read like this:

Materials—10 base sticks of No. 15 cane 17 in long.
        40 (or 39 for the odd number) side stakes of No. 12 cane 27 in long.
        The same number of 4 in bye-stakes for extra strength.
        No. 5 cane for the base weaving.
        No. 6 cane for the siding.
        4 handle liners.
        Approximately 2 yd handle cane.
        Glossy wrapping cane for the handle wrapping.

Make a round base with a diameter of 16 in.

Stake up and upsett with a 4-rod wale for 1 round and continue for 3 more rounds of 3-rod wale.

Bye-stake (see page 5), and insert the handle liners.

Rand for $2\frac{1}{2}$ in and then put on 4 rounds of 3-rod wale.

Trim the bye stakes and nip the side stakes.

Put on a 4-rod border and follow-on trac No. 2.

Remove the handle liners and insert the prepared handle bows.

Tie or nail the bows together and wrap them. Peg the handle to secure.

Example No. 2

Now let us suppose that we want this same basket to be oval, say 20 in $\times$ 12 in. Draw this shape on a piece of paper and measure it. You will find that in this case the circumference is about 53 in. That means that we shall need 42 or 43 stakes at $1\frac{1}{4}$ in apart. We'll choose the 43 as it is more convenient. (If the number of stakes required doesn't fit easily into the base sticks, merely get as near as you can.)

Now we must work out the base sticks from this. As this basket has no flow our base will also measure 12 in $\times$ 20 in.

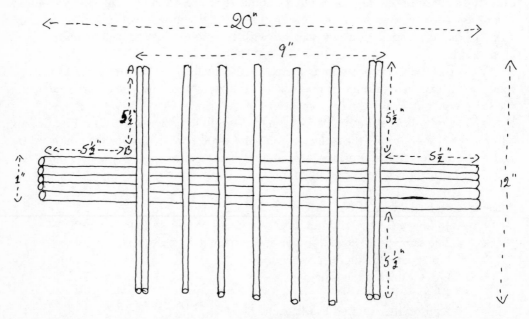

FIGURE 150. HOW TO WORK OUT THE MEASUREMENTS OF AN OVAL BASE

Bearing in mind that A–B and C–B (see Figure 150), must measure the same, and allowing 1 in for the thickness of the long sticks, this means that C–B will be 5½ in at each end. This will leave 9 in in the middle in which to place the short sticks. With 1¼ in between each, and the end ones doubled, you will have 10 short sticks.

Each of the middle short sticks has 1 stake at each end and each of the short sticks at the end has 2 stakes at each end, making a total of 24. As we wanted 43 altogether, you can see that 19 are left to go at the ends beside the long sticks. Each long stick has 2 stakes at each end, therefore we shall need 5 long sticks, and we will be able to leave one stake out to make the odd number.

So our base sticks will be: 5 long sticks of 21 in and 10 short sticks of 13 in, which allows 1 in for ease of working.

The rest of the basket will be completed in exactly the same way as the round one.

I hope you will be able to work out all your oval bases from this example. If you want the basket to flow out, still start with the measurements of the border and calculate the base with the same measurements, but make it up an inch or so smaller all round, and have the short sticks *slightly* closer together. Remember that the stakes at the side of an oval basket do not open out as much as those at the 2 ends.

For a similar basket in squarework, make up the base to the required measurements and the base sticks set 1¼ in apart in the block. Then stake up evenly all round except at the corners where the stakes will be as close as possible.

Always remember that the upsett of a basket will add another ½ in–1½ in (according to the size of the cane or willow) on the diameter or width of your base.

8. Some hints & tips

OVER MANY years of teaching I have 'discovered' many short cuts and useful wrinkles. I hope that they may be of use to you too.

1. When working in willow or hedgerow, keep each set of weavers, i.e. the 2 of a pair, or 3 of a wale, or, say, 23 of a French rand, approximately the same length and size to avoid working a thick rod against a thin and so having uneven work.

2. When staking up a base, always have an odd number of stakes, so that randing or slewing will present no problems later.

3. Always see that the bottom sticks are the thickest of the basket, the side stakes are the next thickest, side weavers a little finer than the side stakes and the base weavers finest of all.

4. Avoid making the base too large, which is a very common fault. Remember that the upsett will put on another 1 in–1½ in on the width of the base of a medium sized basket.

5. Always keep the knife very sharp. You are more likely to cut yourself with a blunt knife because it needs more pressure and is therefore more likely to slip.

6. Remember that basket weaving cannot be pulled tight afterwards—it must be woven into the correct shape.

7. Always pick-off your willow or hedgerow basket as you go, i.e. tidy up the base when that is complete and the upsett when that is done and so on. This is because (a) willow is so much easier to cut when it is mellowed, and (b) the ends are easier to get at, at each completed stage.

8. In willow, waling and pairing should always be started and finished with the tips of the rods to ensure a smooth run in and run out and to avoid a sudden jump, which would leave an ugly gap in the work. (Upsetts may be started with

the butts, but must still finish with the tips.) Waling therefore, having been started with tips and joined in butts to butts, could finish with the 2nd set of weavers, having made approximately 3 rounds. It is much more important to finish with the tips than to have an exact round, finishing where it started. If a larger band of waling is required, work 2 more sets of weavers so that you are back to the tips again.

9. Never have the stakes too close together, there must be sufficient room to pass the weavers between them easily. The thicker the stakes and weavers the larger the space between them must be. Don't forget that the bye-stakes will make the space smaller. If the stakes are too close the work will be very crowded and uneven. It will be necessary to have about 1 in, from centre to centre, when using No. 10 cane.

10. When staking up the base with an odd number, put the single one in where 2 bottom sticks are closest together. The base is very seldom perfectly woven and one nearly always finds that some sticks finish up closer than others. See Figure 133.

11. Make plenty of round baskets before you tackle oval, and plenty of oval before you try square.

12. If the stakes are difficult to insert in square work, use soap to help them slip in.

13. The stakes of square work have a strong tendency to lean and crowd towards the right, therefore hold them well over to the left as the weaving progresses.

14. If a stake cracks during the siding, use a bodkin, or cut a piece of similar sized wood and insert it beside the stake in the manner of a splint. After the weaving has passed the crack, the splint can be removed. If the stake breaks completely, slype the end and insert it beside the existing stake and continue. Don't worry or panic about it—this is quite a common occurence.

15. Do not worry about any stakes that crack on pricking-up. Remove them, re-slype and insert them and try again. Remember that none of the slype must show beyond the edge of the base.

16. Save and carefully keep, all good quality tip ends that you cut off the stakes after the border. Later on, when you want to try some miniature work, these will be invaluable. It is such a waste to 'raid' your bundle and spoil good lengthed rods for such small work.

17. Never open out the bottom sticks too soon. If they are still too crowded after the 5th round, wait another round or two. Remember that the more bottom sticks there are, the more rounds of pairing will be needed before they are all opened out. For instance, with only 6 bottom sticks, they would all be singles after the 3rd round (4th for willow), whereas with 16 or 18 it may take up to 9

or 10 rounds. If you open them out too soon the pairing won't go right down between the sticks and the weaving will be 'gappy'.

Don't make the mistake of thinking that there is a set rule for the number of rounds to be done for each opening—there isn't.

18. Square willow work can be either light or close randed, and there is no doubt that close randing is very beautiful. However, having once decided on a close rand, you must remember to rap down every few rows. Nothing looks worse than a base close randed in parts and light randed in parts. Remember that it takes much longer and much more stuff to close rand.

19. If you require a curve to your basket, e.g. the base, use the natural curve of the willow to help you and arrange the back and the belly in that way.

20. If however, you want your willow to be straight and it isn't, stroke the rod between your thumb and the side of your forefinger, not just where the curve is, but all the way up. Stroke quite firmly, pulling the curve out. Of course, the willow must be prepared for use. 3 or 4 strokes should straighten the rod out. It is a good idea, after the upsett, to see that all the stakes are reasonably straight, and the bottom sticks of a square base may be treated in this way so that you start off with them straight.

21. When you are putting on a trac border in willow which finishes to the inside of the basket, if the ends are rather long, cut them off as you go. This will avoid kinks coming in the wrong places because there isn't room for the rods to lie straight. The same applies to the last round of a French rand as you tuck the tips into the centre.

22. If you can possibly leave your cane long and uncoiled during storage, do so. It is much easier to work with stuff that is straight than stuff that is heavily curled and gets into such a muddle with itself.

23. Do not wale or pair with too long lengths of cane. It gets so twisted up and takes longer in the end. After all, it's easy enough to join in. When working in a busy classroom it's not uncommon to find 2 people using the same piece of cane—one at each end!

24. When making a roll or flower basket with a well splayed out trac border, finish the trac on the *outside* which will be *underneath* the border when it is finished.

25. If you have simply ruined an otherwise good basket with the border, do not throw it away but undo the border and cut off the stakes that are damaged at border level. Try to save 3 or 4 of the originals at different points of the basket, for strength. Slype and insert new stakes well down into the siding, next to, and on the left side, of the original stakes. Prick-down and try again.

26. If you are randing in cane with an *even* number of stakes and therefore you have 2 weavers (see page 29) make sure that they are both roughly as 'kind' as each other. Otherwise the unkind (stiff and unpliable) one will dominate, and the work will become uneven. If you only have 2 weavers left, and one is like wire and the other is like string (not all that unusual) cut each in half so that you do not have to use strong with weak.

27. When starting a round or an oval base, I always find that the easiest and quickest method is to impale the sticks to be pierced, all together on the bodkin. Then the first of the crossway sticks can slip up beside the bodkin. Remove the bodkin and slip the remaining sticks in where the bodkin was.

28. Baskets are measured on the inside for the length and breadth but on the outside for height.

29. The height of a handle of an average shopping basket should be about 7 in from the border. To measure this, lay a ruler (or any stick) across the basket from border to border and then you can measure the handle above that.

30. If your cane basket does need singeing, take great care. Dampen the whole basket first and remember that many a good basket has gone up in flames.

31. To care for your willow or hedgerow basket, leave it out in a summer rain once a year. This washes it, tightens it all up, and puts a little moisture in it, which is so good for it. Both willow and hedgerow will fade in continuous strong sunlight, but this will affect its strength very little. Your well-made willow basket should last 50 to 60 years of constant use.

32. If the handle liners are very difficult to remove, place the basket on the floor with one foot inside, and then pull on the liners with your fingers, or pliers if they are too short to grasp easily. The extra leverage gained by height puts much less strain on both your basket and your temper.

33. Always see that your slype ends in a *real point* or it will get caught up with the weavers as you try to insert it.

34. If your willow basket begins to 'squeak' while you are working it, it means that it is drying out. Pop it under the water for a few minutes and it will quickly re-soak.

35. If you have pricked up the stakes all the way round on the upsett, only to find that you forgot to turn the base over before you started, don't pull all the stakes out in disgust—merely turn them round in their places. The slypes will be the wrong way round, but never mind, remember to turn the base over the next time.

36. Whenever you make a slype for an insertion, always see that the cut side lies next to the stake and is so hidden.

37. If piecing in is necessary in your willow or hedgerow basket, because of a blemish or a broken rod, choose a rod that is the same thickness and will run out with the others. Very often the broken end can be trimmed and re-inserted.

38. Don't make the mistake of thinking that you can put the reverse pair on an oval base merely by turning the base over and working from the other side. This will have absolutely no effect on the twist at all. Reverse pairing must be put on with the upper side of the base facing you and the weavers taken to the back.

39. Don't use willow and hedgerow rods that are too thick. If only thick rods are left, don't hesitate to chop 9 in or 12 in off the butt end. I find that the general tendency is for students to try to use stuff that is far thicker than necessary. It makes the work much harder.

40. Remember the proverb—if at first you don't succeed!!!

9. *Patterns*

(1) WASTE PAPER BASKET IN CANE USING A MANUFACTURED BASE (Figure 151)

Materials: A 7 in or 8 in formica or plywood base
6 oz No. 8 cane for side and bye-stakes
¼ lb No. 5 cane for weaving
2 oz No. 3 cane for decorative weaving
6 yd natural or coloured seagrass

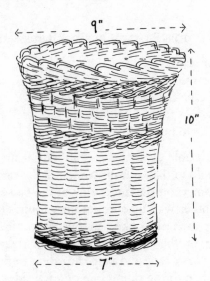

FIGURE 151.

1. Cut 1 side stake for each hole, from No. 8 cane, 20 in long.

2. Soak the stakes at one end (approx. 4 in). Insert the stakes into the holes leaving 4 in protruding from the under side of the base.
3. Work a foot border, using trac No. 3 (see page 36).
4. With No. 5 cane work 4 rounds of waling. (Remember the step-up on each round).
5. Cut 1 bye-stake of No. 8 cane for each stake, 16 in long. Slype and insert them into the waling, one on the right side of each stake.
6. Using No. 5 cane put on $3\frac{1}{2}$ in of randing, and then 4 rounds of waling.
7. With No. 3 cane put on 3 rounds of randing, using 3 strands together, making sure that you don't allow them to twist.
8. Using seagrass, put on 6 or 7 rounds of randing.
9. Repeat instruction No. 7.
10. Work 4 rounds of waling with No. 5 cane.
11. Put on trac border No. 4, still using the double stakes. Turn them down about $1\frac{1}{4}$ in above the border.
12. Pick-off the whole basket. When trimming the border stakes make sure that the ends lie comfortably against each appropriate side stake.

N.B. Instructions 7, 8 and 9 could have been any form of decoration using raffia or strawplait, or a few rounds of pairing or even chain pairing. It could equally well have been continued with plain randing, all according to your own taste.

(2) Small Cane Basket for Easter Eggs or Bridesmaids (Figure 152)

Materials: 2 oz No. 5 cane for stakes
2 oz No. 3 cane for weaving
About 8 ft No. 15 cane for the handle
2 handle liners
An oval wooden base 6 in × 4 in approx.

1. Cut one stake for each hole of the base, 17 in long from No. 5 cane.
2. Put 1 stake in each hole so that 4 in protrudes on the under side.
3. Put on trac border No. 3, on the under side of the basket.
4. Turn the basket the other way up and put on 3 rounds of waling with No. 3.
5. Cut one bye-stake for each side stake 3 in long from No. 5 cane, slype and insert them into the waling, on the right side of each side stake.
6. Rand for $1\frac{1}{2}$ in, with No. 3 cane allowing the siding to flow well out at the ends.
7. Insert the handle liners into the siding one on each side of the basket.
8. Put on 3 rounds of waling.
9. Turn down the stakes and put on a plait border.
10. Remove the handle liners.

11. Cut the No. 15 cane into 4 lengths of 24 in, slype and insert all 4 ends into 1 bow mark.
12. Put on the simple twisted handle described on page 69, using double canes.
13. Secure the handle on each side with a small nail. Pick-off the whole basket.

FIGURE 152.

This little basket is extremely quick and easy to make. For a slightly more elaborate one (Plate 6) work thus:

Follow the instructions to 4.

5. Cut 2 bye-stakes from No. 3 cane, for each side stake and insert them one on *each* side of each side stake.
6. Rand for only 1 in keeping the siding quite straight.
7. Put on 2 rounds of waling.
8. Leave a space of 1 in and put on 1 round of fancy cross fitching, page 26, allowing the siding to flow out at the ends.

9. & 10. As for the 1st basket.

11. Insert a 24 in handle bow of 8 mm cane and wrap it according to the instructions page 62.

12. Peg the handle and pick-off the basket.

(3) CHILDS SMALL ROUND BASKET IN CANE (Figure 153)

Materials: 1 yd No. 10 cane for the base sticks

$\frac{1}{4}$ lb No. 3 cane for the base weaving

$\frac{1}{4}$ lb No. 8 cane for the side and bye-stakes

$\frac{1}{4}$ lb No. 5 cane for the side weaving, and handle

5 yd fine seagrass for the decoration

2 ft 8 mm handle cane

2 handle liners

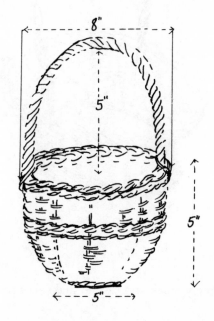

FIGURE 153.

1. Cut 6 base sticks of No. 10 cane, 5 in long, and pierce 3 and thread the other 3 through to form a cross.

2. Tie in the slath and open the sticks out, see page 100. Pair in No. 3 cane to a diameter of $4\frac{1}{2}$ in, making the base slightly concave.

3. Cut and slype 23 stakes of No. 8 cane, 16 in long. Stake up and upsett with one round of 4-rod wale using No. 5 cane. Continue with 3 rounds of 3-rod wale. (See page 105.)

4. Cut 23 bye-stakes 5 in long of No. 5 cane. Slype and insert them into the waling on the right side of each stake.

5. Put on 16 rounds of randing and 1 round of waling, with No. 5 cane, allow the sides to flow out a little.

6. Put on 6 rounds of randing using the fine seagrass.

7. Insert the 2 handle liners on opposite sides of the basket, as far down into the siding as they will go.

8. Put on 1 more round of waling, 10 rounds of randing and then 3 rounds of waling, all in No. 5 cane and keeping the sides vertical.

9. Turn down (nip the stakes) for a 4-rod border and pick-off the basket.

10. Remove the handle liners and prepare, slype and insert the handle bow, as far down as possible.

11. Cut 10 handle canes 26 in long of No. 5 cane, and insert 5 into the border on the left of each end of the handle bow.

12. Rope and finish the handle see page 58. Peg the handle, see page 64.

N.B. Alternative suggestions:

The handle could be wrapped instead of roped, see page 65.

Any decoration, or none could be put in between the 2 single rounds of waling i.e. 3 rounds of flat or enamelled cane, or 1 round of chain pairing using double weavers.

Another attractive decoration is made like this:

Cut off the bye-stakes after the first single round of waling and thread a coloured wooden bead on to each stake except where the handles are to go. Then put on the other single round of waling and re-bye-stake when there is sufficient work to hold them in place.

(4) Lampshades in Cane

Lampshades made in cane are extremely attractive and seem to suit both old cottages and modern houses. They are quick, easy and inexpensive to make, although they are very expensive to buy. They are easily cleaned by a gentle scrubbing in hot water.

The great advantage of making your own, is that you can choose your own size and shape. There are very many possible shapes and instructions for 3 are given here. Once you have made one or two, you will be able to make up your own designs.

Start with the simple straight one to get the 'feel' of them.

Lampshade No. 1 (Figure 154)

Materials: 4 in Lampshade ring, with light fitting, already taped or plastic coated
6 in circle of fairly stout cardboard
1 oz No. 5 cane for the stakes
1 oz No. 3 cane for the waling
1 oz flat cane for the siding

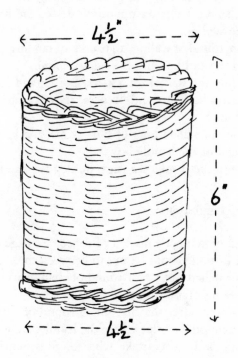

FIGURE 154.

1. Place the ring on the cardboard, and draw round the outside of it.
2. Punch a ring of holes, about ¾ in apart, just outside the drawn circle, making quite sure that you finish up with an odd number of holes (about 17). The holes are quite easy to make with the bodkin.
3. Cut 1 side stake for each hole, 15 in long, of No. 5 cane.
4. Insert a stake into each hole, with 4 in protruding on one side of the cardboard.
5. Put on a foot border using trac No. 3, see page 36.
6. Turn the work the other way up and work 3 rounds of waling in No. 3 cane.***
7. Change to the flat cane and rand for 4 in, keeping the sides quite vertical and

straight. A weight or stone placed inside the shade and resting on the cardboard will make the work steadier and easier.

8. Now work 3 more rounds of waling in No. 3 cane.

9. **** Turn down a 3-rod border and finish with a follow-on trac border, No. 1, taking each stake through the work to the inside.

10. Turn the shade the other way up and undo the foot border. Remove the cardboard ring (if carefully done, it can be used over and over again). Insert the taped light fitting ring and put the foot border down again. Pick off.

N.B. The ring should be a reasonably tight fit, but if it is loose, stitch round in between the cane to hold it fast.

Lampshade No. 2 (Figure 155)

Materials: 4 in Lampshade ring with a light fitting, already taped or plastic coated
6 in circle of fairly stout cardboard
2 oz No. 5 cane for stakes
2 oz No. 3 cane for waling
2 oz Flat cane for siding
3 yd (approx.) Glossy wrapping cane or enamelled wrapping cane of your own choice of colour, for decoration. (The one illustrated was bronze.)

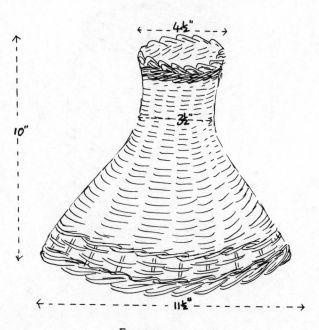

FIGURE 155.

Follow the instructions for shade No. 1 as far as,*** but punch the holes only ½ in apart, making approx. 27, and cut the stakes 23 in long. Closer stakes are needed to start with because of the great flow of the siding.

7. Change to the flat cane and rand for 7 in, at the same time shaping the shade. Weave the siding slightly inwards at first until the work measures 3½ in from the start, and then bring it out quite sharply.

8. Put on 3 rounds of waling in No. 3 cane, 3 rounds of randing in the glossy wrapping or enamelled cane, and 3 more rounds of waling in No. 3 cane.

9. & 10. Finish exactly as for shade No. 1 from.****

Lampshade No. 3 (Figure 156)

Materials: 5 in Lampshade ring, with light fitting, already taped or plastic coated
7 in circle of fairly stout cardboard
2 oz No. 5 cane for stakes
1 oz No. 3 cane for waling
2 oz Flat cane for siding

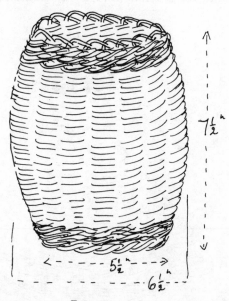

FIGURE 156.

1. Place the ring on the cardboard and draw round the outside of it.

2. Punch a ring of holes, about ¾ in apart, just outside the drawn circle, make sure you finish up with an odd number of holes.

3. Cut 1 stake for each hole, 17 in long, of No. 5 cane.

4. Insert a stake into each hole and put on a foot border, trac No. 3.

5. Turn the shade the other way up and put on 3 rounds of waling in No. 3 cane, already allowing the sides to flow out.

6. Put on 6 in of randing in flat cane, at the same time shaping the shade by flowing it out for the first half of the weaving and back to the original diameter for the 2nd. The barrel shape illustrated increased only 1 in in diameter but you may wish to have yours much more spherical.

7. Finish with trac border No. 3, to make the top and the bottom exactly alike, and complete the shade as before.

N.B. If a very spherical shape is required, you may find it easier to work round a bowl to the half way mark (so that you can remove the bowl) after you have put on the foot border following the instructions on page 166, on how to cover a bowl.

Canework Chain

If your cane work shade is hanging from the ceiling, it will look even more attractive if the flex is semi-concealed in a canework chain. See Plate 8. This chain was also used for the hanging flower basket on page 140. It is an excellent way of using up short, left over pieces of cane. You may be able to think of many other uses for it.

Any sized cane may be used, according to the thickness required.

To make the chain, follow the instructions on page 79 for a Simple Twisted Ring. Then make a second ring, with the first one caught inside when tying the first knot. Finish the second ring as before, moving the first ring round and out of the way all the time. Continue with as many rings as required.

(5) HANGING FLOWER BASKET IN CANE (Figure 157)

Materials: ½ lb No. 11 cane for sticks and stakes
¼ lb No. 5 cane for weaving
¼ lb No. 8 cane for the chain

1. The base and sides of this basket are made all in one. Cut 10 base sticks, of No. 11 cane 32 in long. These will later become the side stakes and then the border stakes.

2. Pierce 5 in the centre and thread the other 5 through them to form a cross.

3. Tie in the slath and open out the sticks, pairing with No. 5 cane, see page 100.

4. Continue to pair with No. 5 cane until the base measures 9 in across, making the base nicely domed; it should now be about 2 in deep.

5. Put on 5 rounds of waling in No. 5 cane.

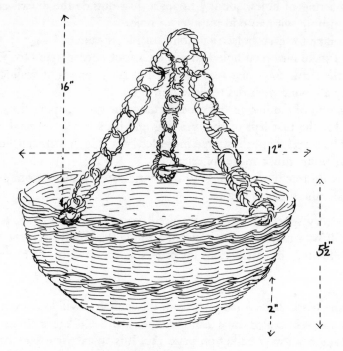

FIGURE 157.

6. Cut 20 stakes of No. 11 cane 12 in long and point each at 1 end.
7. Insert 1 of these stakes into the waling and well down into the pairing of the base, beside, and to the right of each one of the original base sticks ends.
8. Continue to pair with No. 5 cane, opening all the sticks and stakes into singles, at the same time continuing the doming shape. Pair thus for 1½ in.
9. Put on 4 rounds of waling, still bringing the sides of the basket in. It should now measure about 12 in across.
10. Re-soak all the stakes and put on a 3-rod border.
11. Make 3 chains, see page 139, of No. 8 cane and attach to a thicker hanging chain ring.
12. Attach the other end of each chain to the basket, in 3 (equal) places with a thicker ring that passes through the waling of the basket and the last ring of the chain.

(6) OVAL SHOPPING BASKET IN CANE (Figure 158)

Materials: ¼ lb No. 15 cane for the base sticks
¾ lb No. 12 cane for side and bye-stakes

½ lb No. 6 cane for side weaving
¼ lb No. 5 cane for base weaving
3 yd 8 mm handle cane
2 oz No. 6 chair seating cane for handle and base wrapping
6 handle liners

FIGURE 158.

1. Cut 11 base sticks 10 in long and 5 at 15½ in long, of No. 15 cane. Pierce the short ones in the centre and thread the long ones through, and arrange them as shown in Figure 135 on page 109, with the short sticks ¾ in apart.
2. Bind the sticks in place with No. 6 chair seating cane, as shown on page 110.
3. Chain pain the base in No. 5 cane, so that it measures approx. 8½ in × 14½ in, opening the sticks out according to the instruction on page 110.
4. Cut 45 side stakes of No. 12 cane. Slype and insert them, one beside each straight stick to the right, and one each side of the long sticks and the short sticks on the curve, i.e. next to the long sticks, leaving 1 out to make the odd number.
5. Nip the canes at the edge of the base, and tie them into a hoop or bunch.
6. Upsett with 1 completed round of 5-rod wale in No. 6 cane.

7. Put on 4 rounds of 3-rod wale in No. 6 cane, release the hoop or tie and anchor the basket in your favourite way.

8. Cut 45 bye-stakes of No. 12 cane 6 in long. Slype and insert them into the waling, 1 to the right of each stake.

9. Put on 14 rounds of randing in No. 6 cane, allowing the sides to flow very slightly.

10. Put on 1 round of pairing using double weavers, and then 4 rounds of waling.

11. Insert 6 handle liners into the waling—3 equally spaced on each side of the basket.

12. Put on a second round of pairing using double weavers, and then 14 more rounds of randing.

13. Complete the siding with 4 rounds of waling; trim all the protruding bye-stakes close to the waling, and pick off the siding.

14. Nip, and re-soak if necessary, the stakes $\frac{1}{4}$ in above the border and turn down a plait border—see page 46. Pick-off.

15. Prepare 3 handle bows of 8 mm handle cane, well soaked, shaped, and a long slype cut on the inside of the curve. Remove the handle liners and insert the bows as far down into the siding as possible.

16. Nail or sellotape the bows together across the top.

17. Wrap the handle with No. 6 chair seating cane, see page 65.

18. Finish by pegging the handle.

(7) CHRISTMAS BELLS IN CANE
Bell No. 1 (Figure 159)

Materials: $\frac{1}{4}$ lb No. 5 cane for stakes (sticks and stakes are all in one)
2 oz No. 3 cane for weaving

1. Cut 10 sticks of No. 5 cane 39 in long, pierce 5 in the middle and thread the other 5 through.

2. Tie in the slath with No. 3, see page 100, opening the sticks to singles by the 6th round.

3. Continue to pair for another 14 rounds, making the base well domed.

4. Cut 20 bye-stakes of No. 5 cane 18 in long. Slype and insert them, 1 beside each stick. (We will now call them all stakes.)

5. Put on 1 more round of pairing to hold the bye-stakes firmly.

6. Secure the pairing canes by threading them under the weaving of the previous round.

7. Leave a space of 2 in and fitch for 1 round at the same time crossing the stakes over thus; place together the right-hand stake of one pair and the left-hand stake of the next-but-one pair, and fitch round them, repeat this all the way round. Make sure that you always cross them over in the same order.

8. Change to pairing for 2 rounds, then 1 round of fitching.

9. Repeat 7, but allowing the stakes to flow out a little this time. You may prefer the fitch with the extra twist as on page 25.

10. Put on 3 rounds of waling.

11. Finish with trac border No. 4, flowing well out.

12. Add a chain or loop for hanging.

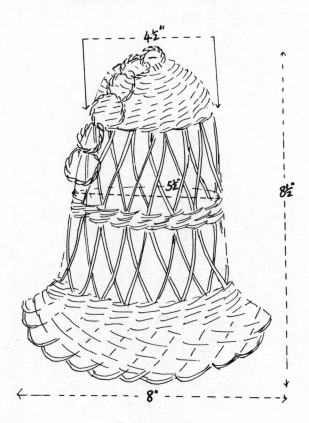

FIGURE 159.

Bell No. 2 (Figure 160)

Materials: 2 oz No. 5 cane for stakes
     1 oz No. 3 cane for weaving

1. Cut 6 sticks (and stakes all in one) 25 in long of No. 5 cane.

2. Make a tiny base as for the first bell with 8 rounds of pairing. Make the base nicely domed.

3. Cut 24 bye-stakes of No. 5 cane and slype and insert them *one on each side* of the base sticks.
4. Put 1 more round of pairing to secure the bye-stakes.
5. Leave a space of 3 in and fitch for 1 round.
6. Wale for 3 rounds.
7. Put on trac border No. 3 using triple stakes, but going from right to left (the opposite way from usual) so that the stakes twist round.
8. Add a ring or loop for hanging.

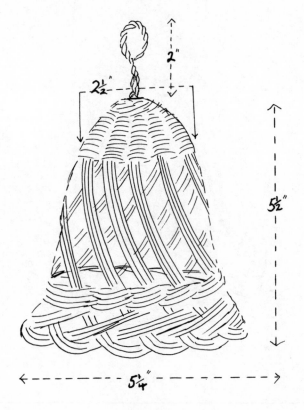

FIGURE 160.

N.B. The 3rd bell in Plate 10 was made from willow. I will leave you to work out the pattern from the picture, except to tell you that the base sticks and the side stakes cannot be made all in one, because of the varying thickness of the rods. Make a small base and add your side-stakes in.

(8) Cornucopia in Cane (Figure 161)

Materials: ¼ lb No. 8 cane for the stakes
¼ lb No. 5 cane for the side weaving
Small quantity of No. 3 cane to start the base weaving

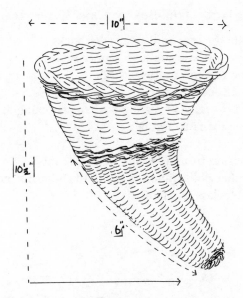

FIGURE 161.

1. Cut 8 sticks 40 in long from No. 8 cane. Make a cross of 4 by 4 and tie in the slath with No. 3 cane, bending the sticks quite sharply at this point to form the end of the horn.
2. Open the sticks out to pairs only (not singles) and continue pairing for 5½ in–6 in keeping the shape very close and 'tubular'. The work should only be about 3 in–4 in across at this point.
3. Now open the sticks to singles and pair for 4 more rounds.
4. Change to No. 5 cane and put on 5 rounds of waling, spreading the stakes out more on 1 side than on the other. We will call the wider side 'the front'.
5. Cut 16 bye-stakes 12 in long of No. 8 cane; slype and insert them into the waling, 1 on the right of each stake.
6. Pair for approx. 15 rounds forming the shape of a horn, i.e. opening out the 'front' and keeping the back fairly straight.
9. Wale for 4 rounds, at the same time opening the stakes out into singles.
10. Nip all these stakes and put on a plait border. Pick-off.

N.B. Having made this one, you will be able to make up your own sizing if you require a larger or smaller horn.

I have also made it in willow and hedgerow stuffs (and of course it looks much more in keeping with the legend). Make it in exactly the same way, but the cross would be made of 10 in–12 in sticks and then side stakes inserted.

(9) Jack-in-the-Box in Cane (Figure 162)

Materials: 4 ft No. 15 cane for base and cover edge sticks
6 ft No. 10 cane for base and lower inner sticks
2 oz No. 8 cane for side and bye-stakes
4 oz No. 3 cane for weaving
Few inches of No. 12 chair seating cane for fastening and hinges
2 in handle cane for fastening peg
Satin lining
9 in approx. Spring from a Hobby or D.I.Y. shop
Golliwog or other doll, stuffed in the head and arms only
A small screwblock is required.

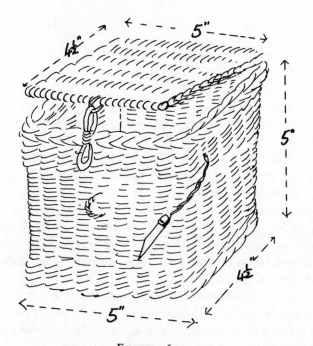

FIGURE 162.

1. Cut 4 base sticks 6 in long from No. 15 cane, and 4 base sticks 6 in long from No. 10 cane, and set them up in the block, with 2 thick ones together on each side and the others evenly spaced inside so that the overall measurement is 4 in.
2. Make the base, weaving with No. 3 cane, according to the instructions on page 113, to a length of 4½ in, finishing with a row of pairing.
3. Cut 28 stakes of No. 8 cane, 11 in long. Slype and insert them, 6 on each of the 2 ends thus: 1 alongside each stake, and 1 *between* the 2 thick sticks at the ends.
4. Slype and insert 8 stakes on each of the 2 long slides, piercing through the thick outer sticks, and placing the end ones as near to the corner as possible.
5. Nip all these stakes and bend them up. Tie together or secure them with an oval hoop.
6. Upsett with No. 3 cane, with a 4-rod wale for 1 round and continue with a 3-rod wale for a further 4 rounds. (Don't forget the step-up each time.)
7. Release the tie or hoop.
8. Cut 8 bye-stakes of No. 8 cane and insert them into the waling, beside each of the 8 corner stakes. (This is to make the corners as square as possible.)
9. Continue to rand, with 2 weavers as there is an even number of stakes (see page 29) with No. 3 cane, to a depth of 3 in, keeping the siding as straight and upright as possible, and keeping the corners as square as you can.
10. Put on a further 4 rounds of waling.
11. Finish the box with a 3-rod border and a follow-on trac, No. 2, so that the border stakes lie in the inside.

The Lid

1. Make a template for the lid, according to the instructions on page 87.
2. Cut 4 outer lid sticks of No. 15 cane and 8 inner sticks of No. 10 cane all about 6 in long. Check with the template that 6 in is long enough.
3. Make the hinge provisions as on page 91.
4. Set all these sticks up in the block to the size of the template, allowing ⅛ in on each side for the randing.
5. Put on the first row of pairing with No. 3 cane and pad the corners if the template is rather rounded. See page 89.
6. Continue to rand in No. 3 cane, making the hinge slots and keeping to the size and shape of the template. Finish with 1 row of pairing.
7. Border each end of the lid, following the instructions on page 92.
8. Make the hinges by wrapping the seating cane round the outer lid stick and 1 cane of the border of the box, 4 or 5 times. Do not cut the cane off after the first hinge but carry it on to the 2nd hinge. Weave the ends away.
9. Make a figure of 8 fastening and attach it to the lid, see page 82.
10. Make a matching twisted loop on the box-see page 80.

11. Make and attach a peg, see page 81.

Line the box with satin to allow the 'Jack' to slip out easily.

Stitch the spring to the bottom of the box, using strong thread and passing it right through and round the base weaving.

Make the 'Jack' with a skirt that will fit over the extended spring.

Stitch the hem of the skirt to the base of the box, again right through the base weaving.

(10) A Round Hat-Box in Cane and Child's Hat (Figures 163 and 164)

Materials: ¼ lb No. 15 cane for the base and cover sticks and fastenings
½ lb No. 12 cane for the side and bye-stakes
¼ lb No. 5 cane for the base and cover weaving
½ lb No. 6 cane for the side weaving
1 oz No. 4 chair seating cane for hinges, fastenings and handle
About 16 in of 8 mm handle cane
About 3 ft of No. 1 cane for the cover stays

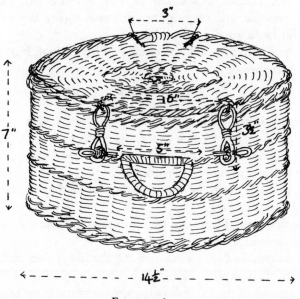

FIGURE 163.

The Box

1. Cut 12 base sticks 15 in long of No. 15 cane, make a cross and tie in the slath, opening the sticks to pairs on the 3rd round, and singles on the 6th or 7th: using No. 5 cane.

2. Continue to pair until the base measures 13½ in, making the shape slightly concave.

3. Cut 47 stakes 22 in long from No. 12 cane; slype and insert them one each side of each stick end except 1, which will only have 1 beside it.

4. Nip the stakes close to the base, bend them up and tie or hoop them into position.

5. Upsett with a single completed round of a 6-rod wale, using No. 6 cane.

6. Put on 4 rounds of 3-rod waling with No. 6 cane.

7. Cut 47 bye-sticks long of No. 12 cane; slype and insert them into the waling one beside and to the right of each side stake.

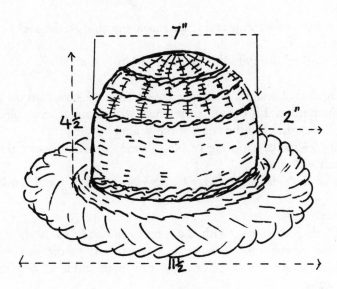

FIGURE 164.

8. Rand for 1½ in with No. 6 cane.

9. Put on 1 round of waling using double weavers of No. 6 cane. Take care not to let the weavers twist over each other but keep them 1 on top of the other all the way round.

10. Put on 7 rounds of randing with No. 6 cane.

11. Repeat 9.

12. Repeat 8.

13. Repeat 6.

14. Trim the bye-stakes level with the top of the waling, and nip the side stakes ready for the border.

15. Put on a 3-rod border and a follow-on trac No. 2, at the same time putting the ends of the border stakes through the basket to lie on the inside. Pick-off.

The Cover or Lid

1. Cut 6 cover sticks 15 in long of No. 15 cane, make a cross and tie in the slath, pairing with No. 5 cane.
2. Continue to pair until the cover measures only 4 in, keeping the weaving quite flat.
3. Put on 1 round of waling using double weavers of No. 5 cane.
4. Pair for 4 more rounds.
5. Cut 24 bye-sticks 6 in long of No. 15 cane; slype and insert them into the 4 rounds of pairing, 1 on *each* side of the cover stick ends. You will now have 36 stick ends in all.
6. Put on 2 rounds of waling, at the same time opening all the sticks out to singles.
7. Pair for 5 rounds.
8. Wale for 1 round using double weavers of No. 5 cane.
9. Repeat 7.
10. Put on 4 rounds of waling, making quite sure that the cover fits the box allowing $\frac{1}{2}$ in for the border, if it doesn't then adjust with more or less waling.
11. Trim the cover sticks to the edge of the waling.
12. Cut 72 border stakes 9 in long of No. 5 cane; slype and insert them 1 on *each* side of each stick end.
13. With the wrong side of the cover facing you, put on a 3-rod border. Pick-off.

The Hinges, Fastenings & the Handle

1. Make a 'D' shaped handle, with the 8 mm cane and No. 4 chair seating cane, following the instructions on page 73, and attach it to the box with 2 twisted loops of No. 5 cane round 2 stakes about 3 in apart, and level with the 2nd round of double waling.
2. Make a hinge of No. 4 chair seating cane round the border of the lid and the border of the box, opposite the handle. Bind the border of the lid with the seating cane first if the borders tend to catch together.
3. Put on a stay hinge, see page 85, of a twist of No. 5 cane, on each side of the hinge, round a stake just inside the waling of the lid to a stake just under the waling of the box.
4. Make 2 figure of 8 shapes, of No. 15 cane and No. 4 chair seating cane, see page 83.
5. Attach each hasp with a twisted loop of No. 5 cane, starting the loop round a stick just inside the border on the outside of the lid and finishing round the same stick on the under side of the lid, so that the loop stands out from the border. Position them 1 each side of the handle.
6. Make 2 fastening pegs of No. 15 cane, see page 82, and attach them to the box with 2 twisted loops of No. 5 cane, positioned so that they correspond with the hasps.

7. Attach 2 8 in twists of No. 1 cane from the lid to the box, one each side, so that the lid is prevented from opening too far.

The Hat

Materials: 2 oz No. 3 cane for the sticks and stakes (all in one)

2 oz No. 1 cane for the weaving

Ribbon and flowers for decoration

1. Cut 10 sticks of No. 3 cane, 30 in long, make a cross and tie in the slath, pairing with No. 1 cane.
2. Pair until the base measures 4 in, with a good concave shape.
3. Put on 2 rounds of waling and a further 4 rounds of pairing, now making the shape quite domed.
4. Cut 20 stakes of No. 3 cane, 13 in long; slype and insert them into the pairing, 1 to the right of each stick.
5. Wale for 2 rounds opening the stakes out to singles.
6. Pair for 6 rounds, continuing with the domed shape.
7. Wale for 2 rounds.
8. Pair for $1\frac{3}{4}$ in and wale for 2 rounds.
9. Commence the brim by upsetting with 1 round of 4-rod waling *on the inside* of the hat, so that the stakes are now at right angles to the crown.
10. Put on 5 rounds of waling on the outside of the hat, with No. 1 cane.
11. Cut 40 border stakes of No. 3 cane 9 in long and insert them into the waling to the right of each stake.
12. Put on a trac border, turning down the stakes approx. $1\frac{1}{4}$ in from the waling, and passing each pair of stakes 'behind 1 and in front of 1' 3 times. Pick-off.
13. Trim with ribbon and/or flowers.

N.B. (1) This hat can be made very much smaller to fit a doll; it looks very attractive and dolly's Mummy is usually very thrilled. Choose No. 1 cane for the stakes and No. 00 for the weaving. (2) The hatbox and hat is very suitable for competition or examination work.

WILLOW BASKET PATTERNS
(11) TEA TRAY IN WILLOW USING A MANUFACTURED BASE

Materials: A manufactured base of any size

A bundle of 2 ft willows (weight will be according to the size of the tray)

Cut out: One side stake for each hole of the base

Quantity of fine weavers

1. Put 1 stake through each hole, inserting the tips through from the wrong side and pulling them as far as they will go. Do not worry if this leaves quite a lot of the rod on the under side.
2. Trim all the stakes to about 4 in on the under side of the tray.
3. Put on trac border No. 3, on the under side of the tray.
4. Turn the tray over and put on approx. 4 rounds of 3-rod waling, starting in 2 different places, with 2 sets of weavers as for the upsett of an oval base, see page 108. If the tray is very large it will be advisable to start in 3 places. Start and finish with the tips of both (or all) sets of weavers.
5. If you are a beginner, prick down and put on a 3 or 4-rod border and cram off following the instructions on page 40, but if you are more experienced put on a 3-rod border with a follow-on 3-rod border, as in Plate 18 Do not cram off at the end of the first border but thread the stakes through as for cane, pull all the stakes back so that they are standing out from the tray at right angles and put on the 2nd border, finishing again as for cane.

(12) Blackberry Basket in Buff Willow (Figure 165)

Materials: 1 lb 3–4 ft English buff willow
Handle bow of ash, hazel, or stout willow. Not too thick as this is a small basket
2 handle liners

Cut out: 10 best fine but long rods for the handle
19 medium thick rods for the side stakes
About 12–16 fine rods for the base weaving
5 bottom sticks 7 in long from the butt ends of fairly stout rods
Upsetting and side weaving rods are taken from the remainder

1. Make a base with the 5 base sticks and the fine weavers, according to the instructions on page 103. Pair until the base measures 6 in across.
2. Pick-off the base and trim the protruding ends of the base sticks.
3. Slype and insert the 19 side stakes, as far into the centre of the base as possible. Prick-up (page 5) and tie the stakes together at the top, or attach a hoop firmly.
4. Upsett with a 4-rod wale for 1 round and continue with a 3-rod wale for about 3 rounds, ending with the tips.
5. Remove the tie, and either fix to a board or anchor with weights.
6. Put on a 2 rod slew for 2 in, allowing the siding to flow out a little.
7. Continue with approx. 3 rounds of waling, beginning and ending with tips.
8. Insert the handle liners, one on each side of the basket.
9. Put on a 3-rod slew, for practice, for a further 2 in.

10. Put on 3 rounds of waling (approx.). Rap down to make sure the siding is an even height all round.
11. Prick-down and put on a 3 or 4-rod border (according to your experience, start with a 3-rod).
12. Remove the handle liners and insert the shaped and slyped bow. Rope the handle according to the instructions on page 58. Secure the handle with a small nail on each side.

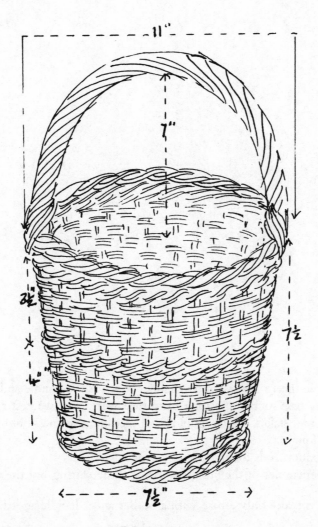

FIGURE 165.

(13) Round Flower Basket in Buff Willow (Figure 166)

Materials: 1 lb Bundle of 4 ft English buff willow
32 in (approx.). Handle bow of ash, hazel, or stout willow
2 handle liners

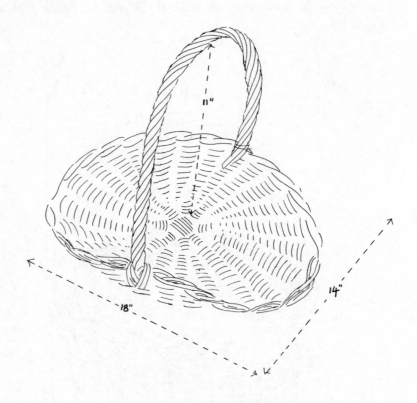

Figure 166.

Cut out: Reserve the 12 longest and yet finest rods for the handle and set them aside
Cut 14 base sticks 15 in long from the butts of the stoutest rods
28 Border stakes, which should be of medium thickness but need only be about
16 in long
12 medium rods for the waling at the edge
The remainder of the bundle is used for the pairing but use the finest first

This basket is really only a base with a border and a handle added.

1. Make a cross of the 14 base sticks, and tie in the slath with pairing, see page 103.

2. Open the sticks out to 2–3–2 after 2 or 3 rounds of pairing but don't attempt to open them out into singles for a further 5 or even 6 rounds.

3. Pair for 5 in, that is 5 in from the centre, trying to shape the basket by bending the 'sides' up but keeping the front and the back flat. It is best to bend the sticks that were slyped rather than the pierced ones. I find that the pierced ones buckle in the middle when they are bent up.

4. If you find it difficult to shape while you are pairing (I'm sure you will at first), tie your basket into shape, across from side to side. Put the string round 2 or 3 sticks on each side, to avoid breaking or distorting them.

5. Add your handle liners now, inserting them into the 'bent up' sides, as far down as possible.

6. Continue with another 2 in of pairing and re-tie the shape at this point if necessary.

7. Put on approximately 3 rounds of waling. Pick off the basket and trim the base sticks level with the edge. Leave the strings in place.

8. Slype and insert 1 border stake beside each stick end, on the left side, with the under side of the basket facing you.

9. Prick the border stakes down and put on a 3-rod border, again with the under side of the basket facing you. See page 40.

10. Remove the handle liners and slype and insert the prepared handle bow. Rope, according to the instructions on page 58.

11. Secure the handle with a small nail through the waling and the bow, at each end.

N.B. (1) Beginners may prefer the simple twisted handle on page 68, in which case, 2 fairly stout willow rods will be required instead of the bow and 12 handle rods. (2) This basket may be made in cane also, using No. 12 for the sticks and No. 5 for the border and the weaving.

(14) Pin Cushion in Willow (Figure 167)

Materials: 55–60 Willow tips (the trimmings from other baskets are ideal)

A small piece of material for the top. Patchwork, embroidery, canvas work can be used to great effect   .

Lining for the sides of the 'cushion'

Sawdust or bran filling

This is really a miniature basket and care must be taken to keep it very fine and dainty. Only use the top 12 in–15 in of each rod. Don't hesitate to cut off any thick ends.

1. Cut 5 base sticks 4 in long, of stuff that is only about $\frac{1}{8}$ in in thickness.

2. Form a cross and tie in the slath, using very fine weavers, according to the instructions on page 103.

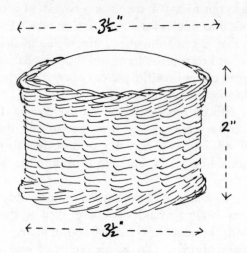

FIGURE 167.

3. Pair to a diameter of 3 in, pick off and trim the protruding base sticks.
4. Slype and insert 19 side stakes, which need not be more than 10 in long.
5. Upsett with a 4-rod wale for 1 round and continue with a 3-rod wale until the 2nd set of weavers runs out.
6. The siding is randed with split willow rods, see page 8, of not more than $\frac{1}{8}$ in thick. Rand for only 1 in, keeping the sides quite straight and upright.
7. Put on approx. 2 rounds of waling.
8. Turn down a 4-rod border, Pick-off.
9. Make a 'cushion' to fit the basket, fill with sawdust, and stitch into position.

N.B. This pin cushion could equally well be made in cane, using No. 5 for the base sticks, No. 3 for the side stakes, and No. 1 for the weavers.

(15) TOY CAT OR DOG BASKET (Figures 168 and 169)

Suitable as it is for Atlas Pattern No. 48, but may be made larger or smaller, according to your own toy pattern.

Materials: 1 lb buff Dicky Meadows (2 ft willow)
2,4 in sticks of either $\frac{3}{8}$ in thick willow or glossy cane

Cut out: 6 base sticks 7 in long
16, approx. finest base weavers
23 side stakes
The remainder is used for the siding

1. Make a round base, not too concave, to a diameter of 5½ in–6 in, pick-off.
2. Stake up with the 23 side stakes, prick-up, and tie the stakes together or put on a hoop.
3. Upsett with a 4-rod wale for 1 round, change to a 3-rod wale for approx. 3 more rounds, until the 2nd set of tips run out.
4. Slew for only ¾ in and then wale for only approx. 2 rounds using shorter rods, and beginning and ending with tips.
5. Insert the 4 in sticks into the siding, each to the left of a stake, and about 4 in apart. This forms the opening, which will now be bordered down with a 3-rod border.

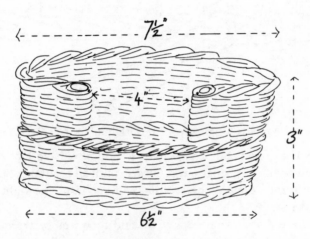

FIGURE 168.

6. Insert an extra border stake, beside the stake one to the left, of the left-hand stick that you have just inserted. See Figure 169.
7. Twist a rod round the stick, and the adjoining stake, so that both ends protrude to the front. For the sake of clarity we will number these ends 1—6. (Figure 169.)
8. Take 1 over and in front of 3, and the stick, and behind 5, out to the front to lie in front of 6.
9. Bend 3 down to lie beside and behind.
10. Take 2 in front of 5, behind 6 and out to the front to lie in front of 7.
11. Bend 5 down to lie beside and behind 2.
12. Take 4 in front of 6, behind 7, and out to the front to lie in front of 8.

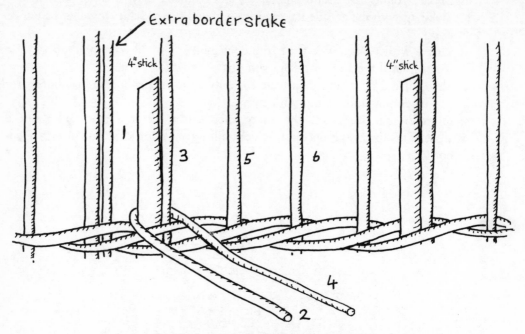

FIGURE 169. THE BORDER OF THE OPENING OF THE CAT BASKET

13. Bend down 6 to lie beside and behind 4. You now have 3 pairs to the front and can continue with a normal 3-rod border, until all the stakes between the 2 sticks have been turned down. The last one will go *behind* the right stick. Pick off all these border stakes.

14. Continue now by slewing backwards and forwards between and round the 2 thick sticks for a further 1 in. Keep the weavers in order as they go round the sticks and do not let them twist over.

15. Put on 1 round of waling. Start at the left side by bending a rod round the stick to form 2 ends and add in the 3rd weaver. Twist *one* of these rods round the stick at the other end.

16. Put on a 3-rod border, starting and finishing in exactly the same way as for the border of a square lid, page 92, except that your border stakes are already in place and you only need to add one stake to the front of the thick stick, which is bent down in front and the 8 in rod wrapped round the sticks.

    Make a cushion for the basket (I made mine in pale blue satin with Italian quilting), and a kitten from Atlas transfer No. 48.

N.B. This basket could be made just as easily in cane, even using a manufactured base to start with.

(16) ROUND SHOPPING BASKET IN BUFF & WHITE WILLOW (Figure 170)

Materials: 1 lb 4 ft English buff willows
$\frac{1}{2}$ lb 3 ft English white willows
34 in (approx.) handle bow of ash or hazel
2 handle liners of 8 in–9 in

Cut out: 12 best long but fine rods for the handle
23 medium thick rods for side stakes
About 16–20 small fine rods for the base weaving
6 base sticks 8$\frac{1}{2}$ in long from the butts of the stoutest rods
The remainder of the buff rods and the white rods are used for the upsetting and the siding

1. Make a cross with the 6 base sticks, tie in the slath and open the sticks, according to the instructions on page 103.

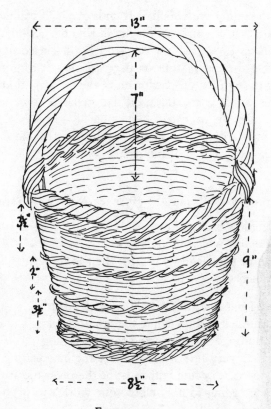

FIGURE 170.

2. Continue pairing until the base measures 7 in, making it slightly concave.
3. Pick off the base and trim the protruding ends of the base sticks.
4. Slype and insert the 23 side stakes, as far into the centre of the base as possible, prick-up (page 5) and tie the stakes together at the top, or attach a hoop firmly.
5. Upsett with a 4-rod wale for 1 round and continue with a 3-rod wale for about 4 rounds, ending with the tips.
6. Remove the tie or hoop and fix firmly to the workboard or anchor with weights.
7. Put a band of French waling with 23 rods of white willow, allowing the siding to flow out a little.
8. Change to buff willow. Put on 1 round of waling, keeping the rods a uniform thickness by starting with the butts and joining in new rods $\frac{1}{2}$ way round. Finish this round off as you would for cane, see page 18.
9. Insert the handle liners on opposite sides of the basket for a single bow.
10. Put on a small band of French randing with very fine buff rods, for about $1\frac{1}{2}$ in.
11. Repeat 8.
12. Repeat 7.
13. Complete the siding with about 4 rounds of 3-rod waling. Rap down the siding to make sure that it is an even height all round. Pick-off the siding.
14. Prick the stakes down for a 4 or 5-rod border, according to your experience, and following the instructions on page 40. (Don't forget to see that your stakes are mellow enough for the hard bend of the border—if not, re-soak for a while.)
15. Remove the handle liners and insert the prepared bow.
16. Rope the handle, see page 58.
17. Secure the bow with a small nail through 1 or 2 of the waling rods and into the handle bow, on each side of the basket.

(17) Oval Shopping Basket in Buff & White Willow (Figure 171)

Materials: $\frac{1}{2}$ lb 4 ft English buff willows
$\frac{1}{2}$ lb 4 ft English white willows
Ash, hazel, or stout willow rod for the handle
2 handle liners

Cut out: 12 best long but fine rods of white for the handle
33 medium thick rods of white for the side stakes
26 White rods for the upsett and the top waling
Approx. 8–12 very fine white rods for the base pairing
Approx. 16–20 very fine buff rods for the reverse pairing
Approx. (according to how close your work is) 25–35 medium fine buff rods for the siding

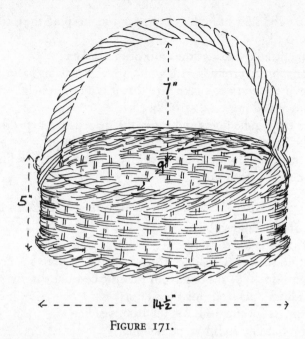

FIGURE 171.

7 base sticks 9 in long ⎫
4 base sticks 14 in long ⎬ Cut from fairly sturdy butt ends

1. Make a slath of the bottom sticks, arranged as shown on page 109, with the short sticks 1¼ in apart.
2. Tie in the slath with the fine white base weavers, i.e. to start the pairing and continue up to the point where all the sticks are opened out.
3. Continue to pair with the fine white rods for a little less than ½ the base.
4. Change to the fine buff weavers and REVERSE pair for half the base.
5. Still using the buff weavers revert to the pairing for the last few rounds. The base should now measure 13 in × 8 in. Pick off.
6. Stake up with the 33 white side stakes thus: 1 stake beside each straight short stick ends, 1 stake on *each side* of the long stick ends, 1 stake on *each side* of the curved short stick ends. Remember to leave 1 out, where the sticks are closest, to give an odd number.
7. Prick-up the stakes and tie up or put on a hoop.
8. Upsett with a 4-rod wale, using 2 sets of white weavers, starting at opposite ends of the basket. See page 108.
9. Change to a 3-rod wale after the first round, finishing with the tips of the 2nd set of weavers.
10. Release the tie and secure the basket in your favourite way.

11. Put on a 2-rod slew of buff weavers for 3 in, keeping the siding quite straight and upright.
12. Put in the handle liners at the ends of the basket.
13. Wale for approx. 3 rounds with white weavers, starting as for the upsett in 2 places.
14. Rap down the work to make sure that it is an even height all the way round.
15. Prick down and put on a 4-rod border.
16. Remove the handle liners and insert the shaped and slyped handle bow.
17. Rope the handle, following the instructions on page 58.
18. Secure the handle with a few small nails through the waling rods and into the handle bow, on each side.

(18) DOLL'S CRADLE IN BUFF WILLOW (Figure 172)

Materials: 1 lb 4 ft–5 ft English buff willow
 1 pair of wooden rockers
Cut out: 4 bottom sticks 13½ in long from the sturdiest butts in the bundle
 7 bottom sticks 8½ in long from the sturdiest butts in the bundle
 33 medium thick rods for the side stakes
 Approx. 24–28 fine rods for the base weaving
 12 long but fine rods for the fitching
 33 bye stakes, roughly the same thickness as the side stakes between 6 in and 10 in long. (You can probably collect these from the cut off pieces from other baskets.)

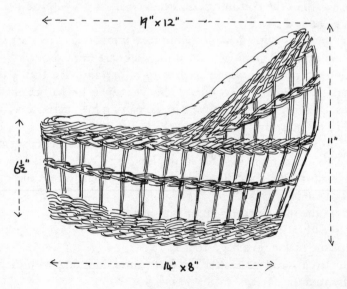

FIGURE 172.

1. Make an oval base with the base sticks and fine base weavers to a size of 13 in × 7 in

2. Upsett with a 4-rod wale for 1 round, starting with 2 sets of weavers, on opposite sides of the basket.

3. Continue to 3-rod wale for approx. 6 rounds, finishing with the tips of both sets of weavers.

4. Bye-stake with the 33 odd pieces, arranging them so that the basket is higher at the head than at the foot. Start the rise just after halfway along the side.

5. Leave a space of 1 in and fitch for 1 round. If you find it difficult to fitch with willow, fitch first with a piece of cane which can be cut away later. Allow the siding to flow out a little.

6. Pair for 1 round.

7. Repeat 5.

8. Wale for 1 round.

9. Put on a *row* of fitching at the head of the cradle, using only the top 16 stakes (or 15 if you left your odd stake out here). Start with the fitching touching the last waling round and allow it to rise up at the middle of the head to $1\frac{1}{2}$ in and drop down to touch the waling on the other side.

10. Put on a row of pairing over these same stakes.

11. Repeat 9.

12. Put on approx. 3 rounds of 3-rod waling right round the cradle, starting as for the upsett, in 2 places and finishing with the tips of both sets of weavers. Keep the shape correct.

13. Prick down and put on a 3-rod border. *Don't* cram off but thread the last rods through as you would for cane.

14. Finish with a follow-on 3-rod border. Don't attempt this last border until you are experienced, but if it goes hopelessly wrong you can cut the stakes off just under the first border and not much harm is done. Pick-off.

Screw on the rockers (you can get these from a D.I.Y. shop), and thoroughly enjoy making the fitted mattress and bed linen. I found that the little pillow looks and fits better if it is 'D' shaped, rather than rectangular.

(19) Bird Cage in White Willow & Palembang (Figure 173)
(As this cage is a rather advanced piece of work, I have kept the usual instructions to a minimum.)

Materials: 1 lb 4 ft–5 ft white willow
            $\frac{1}{4}$ lb 3–5 mm palembang cane, using the finest canes you can find

Cut out: 8 base sticks 15 in long from the butts of the sturdiest rods
           8 'crown' sticks 7 in long from the butts of the next sturdiest rods

32 stakes of medium thickness
Approx. 12–16 fine weavers for the 'crown'
Approx. 20–24 fine weavers for the base
5 door sticks, about 5 in long, not as thick as the stakes
16 very fine weavers for the door (you could use the tips cut from the stakes)
Palembang cane for the fitching

1. Make a base with the 15 in sticks to a diameter of approx. 10 in and set it to one side.
2. Make a 'crown' in exactly the same way as a base, with the 7 in sticks, with a fairly deep concave shape, to a diameter of approx. 6 in.

FIGURE 173.

3. Cut the stakes so that they measure about 25 in; cut any very thick butts off, but otherwise cut the necessary length off the tip, so that a fairly sturdy end is left to go into the 'crown'.

4. Slype and insert these stakes into the 'crown' one on each side of each stick end.

5. Secure each one with a small nail, through a pairing rod and into the stake, on the inside of the 'crown'.

6. Hoop the stakes at the butts with a wide hoop.

7. Leave a space of $2\frac{1}{2}$ in and put on 1 round of fitching with the palembang.

8. Put on 1 round of pairing with the palembang.

9. Draw in the hoop a little, to make the cage a good shape, and repeat 7 and 8.

10. Draw in the hoop still further, so that the next round of fitching is almost the same diameter as the last, and leaving a space of $3\frac{1}{2}$ in this time, repeat 7 and 8.

11. Repeat 7, keeping this round exactly the same diameter as the previous round.

12. Put on approx. 2 rounds of waling.

13. Measure the base to see if it fits well into the waling. If it is too small, add a little more pairing, and if it is too big then take a little off. When you are satisfied with the fit, prick-up the protruding stick ends, with the under side of the base uppermost.

14. Fit the base into the waling of the cage. There will be 1 stick end to 2 stakes and a little manoeuvring will soon determine the best way to place it.

15. Put on approx. 3 more rounds of waling bending the base sticks up so that they lie with, and are woven in with the side stakes.

16. Complete the cage with trac border No. 2.

The Opening & Door

1. Cut 3 consecutive stakes in the middle of the 3rd space, and shave the rod away on the outside, leaving a 'skein' on the inside. Repeat with all 6 ends.

2. Soak these ends for a few minutes to make sure they are 'kind', then twist each one in turn, over and into the weaving of the fitching below or above, until the end is lost.

3. Set the door sticks up in the screwblock so that the outer sticks just cover the edge sticks of the 'gap'.

4. Make the door in the usual way for squarework, bordered off top and bottom, so that it fits exactly into the opening.

5. Make a hasp of twisted willow at the top of the door so that it protrudes from the border.

6. Make a hinge at the bottom of the door, in 2 places (the 2 centre spaces are best), using a willow or palembang skein, and going right round the fitching and pairing.

7. Make a loop of twisted willow, in the fitching at the top of the door, to fit the hasp of the door.
8. Make and attach a peg according to the instructions on page 81.
9. Complete the cage with a hanging ring at the top, I used a simple twisted ring of palembang, attached by binding with a palembang skein 3 times into the cross of the 'crown'.
10. Make a perch if desired, with a fairly stout rod, pricked down in 2 places so that the centre section fits across the cage (like the gauge on page 117). Insert the 2 ends into the fitching and pairing. Make a toy bird if desired, or use your cage as a plant holder.

N.B. This basket is very suitable for exhibition or examination work.

(20) To Make a Cover for a Bowl, Pot or Bottle

Materials: Any stuff that you may wish to use, making sure that you keep it very fine in relation to the size required. Skein work is particularly useful here.
1. Use the methods of planning in the chapter on designing, to find out how many base sticks are required.
2. Make up the base to the required size and shape, making quite sure that it is not too large, but only just fits the bottom of the article to be covered. Remember that the upsett will make the base quite a bit larger.
3. Stake up, and upsett with only 1–2 rounds of waling.
4. Tie the base, very securely, to the article to be covered. Use string, and sellotape, if necessary.
5. Continue with the upsett now, to the depth required.
6. Put on any suitable siding weaves, keeping very close to the article, following the curves in or out.
7. If there are any handles to put on the side, it is easier to put them on when the siding is at the required position rather than adding them later. Especially if the foundation is not to be removed, as in the case of a bottle.
8. Any of the borders are suitable. The shape of the article may determine the type of border. A bottle is well bordered by using trac No. 1 (behind one, instead of in front of one) and a follow-on plait round the bottle. In Plate 17, 1 bowl has a 4-rod border, 1 has a 3-rod with a back-trac of trac No. 2, TWICE, and the 3rd is bordered with trac No. 3.

10. The Basket Maker's Dictionary

BACK	The convex side of a willow rod.
BACK-TRAC BORDER	A border put on after another border, but going in the opposite direction.
BASE	The bottom of the basket.
BASKET	One of many names given to a receptacle of woven wood or grasses etc.
BELLY	The natural concave side of a willow rod—opposite the back.
BODKIN	A sharp piercing tool (the true use of the word bodkin).
BOLT	Commercial willow is sold by the bolt or bundle. It is a girth measurement of 37 in, 8-12 in up from the butts.
BORDER	The decorative edge of a cover or basket.
BOW	The foundation of a handle.
BOW-MARK	The space left open in the siding, by a handle liner, to take the bow.
BRIDGE	A piece of work, usually randing, put in to make a partition inside the basket or across the top to attach a cover.
BROWN	Commercial willow that is dried with the bark on.
BUFF	Commercial willow that is boiled with the bark on and then stripped and dried.
BUNDLE	See bolt.
BUTT	The thick end of the willow rod.
BYE-STAKE	A second stake inserted beside the main stake for extra strength.
CANE	Also Pith Cane, Centre Cane, Pulp Cane. Of the rattan family and imported from Asia. Factory processed to obtain uniform thickness.
CHAIN PAIR	One round of pairing and one round of reverse pairing.

CHAIR SEATING CANE	A fine wrapping cane taken from the outer covering of centre cane.
COMMANDER	A tool for softening willow rods in preparation for making hasps and nooses.
COVER	The basket maker's name for a lid.
CLEAVE	A tool for splitting willow into 3 or 4 skeins.
CLOSE RAND	Randing that is repeatedly knocked down with the rapping iron to produce tight, close work.
CLUNG	Stuff that has been partially dried, as in hedgerow woods that are ready to use.
CRAM–OFF	The method used to finish a rod border in willow or hedgerow.
CREEL	A regional name for a basket.
CROSS	The start of a round base (see page 100).
CROSS HANDLE	The type of handle that goes right across a basket and is usually wrapped or roped.
CUTTING OUT	Term used for grading the stuff into sizes, suitable for the various parts of the basket.
DICKY MEADOW	Term used for the smallest of all willow, about 2 ft.
ENAMELLED CANE	Coloured wrapping cane.
ENGLISH RAND	One of the weaves suitable for willow and hedgerow.
FITCH	A type of weave, used after a space, which grips the stakes firmly (see page 24).
FLOW OR SPRING	The difference in size between the bottom and the top of the basket.
FOLLOW-ON BORDER	A border that is put on after another one, and going in the same direction.
FOOT OR FOOTING	An extra piece of work added to the bottom of a basket. The plural of foot is foots.
FOOT BORDER	The border added to the foot, or the border used with a wooden base.
FRENCH RAND	Weaving suitable for willow and hedgerow (see page 29).
FRENCH SLEW	Like French randing but using double weavers.
GLOSSY CANE	A whole cane that is not stripped of its hard outer covering. Used for furniture and the handles of baskets.
GLOSSY WRAPPING CANE	The hard outer covering of centre cane, used for wrapping handles.
GREAT	Term used for the largest willow, 8 ft–6 in to 10 ft in length.
GREEN	Willow (or hedgerow woods) before it is dried, regardless of colour.
GRIN	Spaces that may occur in a roped handle.

HANDLES	That part of the basket by which it is held. Main types of handles are cross and small.
HASP	Part of the fastening on a basket.
HINGE	Used to attach a cover and usually made of twisted or plaited willow or cane or a skein.
HOOP	A band attached to the stakes during the upsetting, to keep them in the shape required.
	Or, the foundation of scallom work.
HULLINGS	Green willow of 4 ft length.
KIND	A very pliable piece of stuff, easy to use.
LAP-BOARD	A work board held in the lap with the basket attached (see page 3).
LAPPING OR WRAPPING	Willow skein or glossy wrapping or chair seating cane used for binding the handle bow or the slath of an oval cane basket.
LEADER	A rod or skein taken across a handle and wrapped over and under to form a pattern (see page 61).
LEAGUE	A bottom stick which continues on to become a stake.
LIGHT RAND	Randing that is just touching—the opposite of a close rand.
LINER OR REPRESENTATIVE	A piece of cane or willow, inserted beside a stake to keep a space open, e.g. Handle liner (see page 57).
LISTING	Additional decorative skein work on a wrapped handle.
LONG SMALL	Term used for 5 ft willow rods.
LUKE	Term used for 4 ft willow rods.
MIDDLESBORO'	Term used for 7 ft to 8 ft willow rods.
MACKERELL BACK	Medium quality whole cane.
NOOSE	Part of the fastening on a basket.
OSIER	Regional name given to willow grown specially for basket making, usually *salix viminalis*. Used in East Anglia and the Midlands and sometimes in the Home Counties.
OVAL	One of the most common shapes of a basket, determined by its base.
PAIR, PAIRING	Type of weaving with two weavers, used mostly for bases.
PALEMBANG	A whole cane of the rattan family. Needs a lot of soaking and is often very unkind.
PEG	Part of the fastening of a basket (see page 82).
	Or, the plug put in the bow of a cross handle to prevent the handle slipping out.
PICK-OFF	The act of tidying a basket by trimming the unwanted protruding ends. Should be cut off with a slanting cut.

PICKING KNIFE   Knife used for picking-off.

PIECE IN   Joining in a new rod when the old one runs out or breaks.

PITH OR PULP CANE   See cane.

PLAIT   One of the borders. There are many variations.

PLANK   Workboard held from the floor to the knee with the basket attached for working.

PRICK RAND   A method of commencing randing by inserting the rods into the work. Used when no protruding ends are wanted.

PRICK-UP   Method used to turn willow or hedgerow stakes at the upsett without cracking them (see page 5).

PRICK-DOWN   As prick-up but at the border.

RAGGED   Roughest of all the willow rods and only used for the bottom or coarse work.

RAND   Type of weaving using only one weaver (see page 27).

RAPPING IRON   Tool used for knocking the work down to level it up or for close randing.

REPRESENTATIVE   See Liners.

REVERSE PAIR   A weave using two weavers (see page 23).

RIB RAND   A fancy weave using only one weaver.

ROD   Name given to one piece of willow.

ROD BORDER   The most common border.

ROPE BORDER   Type of border used extensively on the Continent.

ROPE HANDLE   A handle with a bow and covered with rods or canes to give an effect of rope (see page 58).

ROMAN   To put the Roman in is to slew with 5, 6 or even more rods for very quick work.

ROUND   One complete round of work.
Or, the most common and easiest shape for basketry, determined by the base.

ROUND NOSED PLIERS   Tool used for nipping cane to make it bend more easily at the upsett or border.

SALIX   Latin name for willow. Commercial varieties are: *Salix Viminalis*, *Salix Purpurea*, and *Salix Triandra*.

SCALLOM   A method of staking up by looping the butt ends, well slyped, on to a hoop.

SCREWBLOCK   Tool used for making square bases and covers.

SHAVE   Tool used in the making of skeins.

SHEARS   Tool used for cutting.

SHORT NATURE   The best and kindest whole cane.

SHORT SMALL   Term used for 4 ft willow rods.

SHRIPPED UP	Coarse rods that have had their side shoots removed.
SIDE CUTTERS	Tool used for cutting cane only.
SIDING	The weaving on the side of the basket.
SKEIN	Willow that has been split and trimmed and is used for lapping. Skeinwork—weaving with skeins.
SLATH	The bottom sticks of an oval or round base when they are tied together and first opened out. This is called tying in the slath.
SLEW	A type of weave for willow or hedgerow (see page 33).
SLYPE	The method used for cutting the butts of a willow rod (see page 5).
SPRING	See flow.
SQUARE	One of the basket shapes and refers to the right angled corners of the base (see page 112).
SQUEAKY	Willow that is too dry for use and needs wetting. Or, the most unkind of the whole canes.
STAKE	Rod of thickish willow or cane which forms the framework of the side.
STAKE UP	The act of inserting the stakes into the base and prior to the upsett.
STEP–UP	A stroke used on each round of waling to avoid a spiral look. Used only with cane or stuff of uniform size.
STICKS	Short thick lengths of willow or cane used for the foundation of a base or cover.
STUFF	Any material that the basketmaker may be using.
TACKS	Term used for 3 ft willow rods.
THREEPENNY	Term used for 6 ft willow rods.
TIP OR TOP	The small thin end of a willow rod.
TRAC OR TRACK	One of the borders, has many variations (see page 35).
UNKIND	Stuff that is difficult to use, the opposite of kind.
UPRIGHT	Tool used in the making of willow skeins.
UPSETT	The rounds of weaving, usually waling, put on after the stakes have been turned up, and which change the work from going out to going up. P.P. of upsett is upsetted.
VALE	A border that looks like a plait but is put on in a different way. More commonly used in soft basketry.
WALE	A weave using three or more weavers (see page 15).
WEAVER	A rod or piece of cane that is used for weaving.
WICKER	Name for willow basketry.
WITHY	Regional name for willow that is grown specially for the basket trade. Used in the West Country.